Phenomenology's Material Presence:
Video, Vision and Experience

Gabrielle A. Hezekiah

intellect Bristol, UK / Chicago, USA

First published in the UK in 2010 by Intellect,
The Mill, Parnall Road, Fishponds, Bristol, BS16 3JG, UK

First published in the USA in 2010 by Intellect, The University of Chicago Press,
1427 E. 60th Street, Chicago, IL 60637, USA

Cover stills from *Journey to Ganga Mai.* Courtesy the artist.

A catalogue record for this book is available from the British Library.

Cover design: Holly Rose
Copy-editor: Jennifer Alluisi
Typesetting: John Teehan

ISBN: 978-1-84150-310-3

Printed and bound in Great Britain by 4edge Ltd, Hockley. www.4edge.co.uk

Contents

PREFACE

This book is an exploration of phenomenology and the aesthetics of the moving image. It is a meditation on three videos by Trinidadian artist Robert Yao Ramesar and the overlapping aims and strategies of philosophy and experimental documentary. The principal questions are these: How does video make visible the act of looking and the act of being seen? How does it intimate the presence of that which cannot be seen? And what is the role of video's material body in facilitating this process? The book is about the process of inquiry that properly belongs to the videos and the *call* of the videos to our own consciousness.

I have come to these questions through an indirect route. These videos offer a number of possibilities for examining questions of identity and representation in a postcolonial context—for analyzing the ways in which they might subvert or reinforce dominant tropes and techniques of ethnographic filmmaking. Initially, I was attracted by such possibilities. Yet Ramesar's work offers much more than this. In its attention to the *process* and *experience* of visibility, it moves beyond questions of representation and towards a poetics of seeing and becoming. Ramesar's work is lyrical and evocative. It brings the viewer into *contact* with the object being viewed and at the same time evokes the spectre of unseen presence. It challenges the viewer to interrogate the very process of vision that brings the videos' objects towards us—and the process through which vision is "made." My initial attempts at deconstruction seemed misplaced. They seemed to run counter to the spirit of the work and to my experience of it. They appeared to force an external reality onto the reality that was continually—and already so eloquently—revealed by the videos themselves. The critical approaches that I had explored up to that point could not reproduce the experience of encounter.

The videos drew attention to their own materiality as audiovisual objects—and to the implications of this materiality for the possibility of knowledge. Ramesar's techniques of slow motion and depixellation *lengthened* time and *created* gaps. In the lengthening of time, I was forced to contemplate. In the creation of physical gaps, I was allowed to enter—and to have video's objects move towards me. Ramesar's videos invited a kind of congress—a joining that could not easily be avoided, a joining that could not easily be explained. It became impossible to talk or write *around* the videos rather than *into* and *towards* them. The experience of contact—and the intensity of that contact—demanded to be addressed. Video and its objects—the objects that video as a medium brought towards me—were about the business of presenting themselves to and for my vision, of ensuring that I *received* them. They seemed to suggest that there was something beyond mere appearance that it was possible to know: that true apprehension existed somehow on the hither side of what I had come to understand as representation.

There are few theoretical approaches that can adequately account for the experience of encounter initiated by this work. Approaches based on poststructuralist frameworks are typically discursive rather than experiential—they reduce film to a text to be read rather than an object to be apprehended. They fail to account for the fullness of contact with the materiality of film and are inadequate to engage productively with the *visual encounter* that is Ramesar's video production. The distinction between the look of a film and the look that properly *belongs* to the film is not generally made. In his discussion of the production and viewing experience, ethnographic film-maker and theorist David MacDougall begins to address the question of encounter in documentary cinema. MacDougall is interested in our consciousness of a certain "something" in the filmed documentary subject—the person filmed—that I believe might be interpreted as a form of excess. He writes of the ways in which film might retain a trace of embodied presence and the process through which that presence is partially lost. That presence exists beyond textual analysis. MacDougall is interested in a form of consciousness, rather than meaning or signification, that is presented to us in a film and the ways in which that consciousness can return us partially to the life of the subject so truncated by the act of selection that takes place in editing. He suggests that it is only "by denying representation, by breaking through its plausibility" that film can "contrive to heal the wound that cinema creates and so restore the viewer to the world" (MacDougall 1998: 49). It is this notion of restoration to the world that began to guide my own journey. I came to see my experience of viewing more clearly as an experience of a world co-constituted by video and by my presence as a viewer of it. This restored a level of subjectivity to my own inquiry and I turned to phenomenology as a way of addressing these issues.

In this way, the project became not an argument, but a meditation and an exploration. It was a movement into, alongside and with an idea: that video might offer a point of access to a world where consciousness met to produce knowledge of presence. This exploration took me to theorists who have used phenomenology to expand on their interpretation of film and also to the philosophers of phenomenology themselves. Here I found experience, subjectivity and presence combined in a profound and palpable investigation of the world. It became clear to me that the videos' performance mirrored the investigation of the philosophers, and that this project was essentially about writing into that relationship and experience. I have returned, therefore, to the *methods* of the phenomenologists in an effort to make clear these connections. At the same time, I have attempted to follow the videos' own intentions and to engage readers in the experience of consciousness and encounter so central to the viewing of Ramesar's work.

Phenomenology's Material Presence is an experimental essay that is intended to make consciousness the focus of an inquiry. It is an attempt to create new forms of writing that might do justice to the videos and to my encounter with them. Academic writing typically imposes theorizing upon the moving image and the moment of vision is lost. This book is an attempt to "see phenomenologically"—connections, intention and consciousness—and to dwell with the experience of looking as an act of theorizing. I make use of phenomenology as a framework for understanding video's intention and as a method for staying with the trace of the viewing experience. This work is an attempt to dwell with an experience of contact through an act of continually unfolding reflection.

Acknowledgements

As always in a project of this nature, I am indebted to many, but I will mention only a few here. This book began as a doctoral project, and I would like to thank the members of my supervisory and examination committees—Kari Dehli, Rinaldo Walcott, Laura U. Marks, Roger I. Simon and Janine Marchessault—for the extraordinary attention that they paid to the intellectual value of the work. They showed unwavering support for what turned out to be an unorthodox piece of writing within the context of academia. In particular, I would like to thank my supervisor, Kari Dehli, for her clear and steady guidance, and Laura U. Marks for her generosity and her interest in seeing this work come to publication. Sherene H. Razack took me through the early stages of this process and Frederick I. Case continues to cheer me on from the great beyond. Kristine Pearson and Margaret Brennan deserve special mention for helping me to navigate the administrative world of graduate studies. Research for this project was made possible through a Social Sciences and Humanities Research Council Doctoral Fellowship and an Ontario Graduate Scholarship while I was at the University of Toronto.

Several academic departments outside of my home institution also facilitated my research and writing. I would like to thank Faye Ginsburg of the Department of Anthropology and the Center for Media, Culture and History at New York University. My time as a Visiting Scholar at the Universitat de Barcelona in the Masters and Postgraduate Programme for the Study of Visual Culture was very productive in allowing me to think through the transition from thesis to monograph. For their warm welcome, I would particularly like to thank Aida Sánchez de Serdio, Carla Padró, Judit Vidiella, Paola Cinquina, José María Barragán and Fernando Hernández.

I was very fortunate to have received the love and support of numerous friends and family members throughout this process. They cannot all be listed here but I must mention my gratitude to my parents, Molly Hezekiah, Randolph Hezekiah and June Hezekiah. Thank you also to Maureen Edwards, Cameron Bailey, Ojelanki K. Ngwenyama, Ernest Massiah, Logan Brenzel, Deborah Root, Anne-Marie Stewart, Honor Ford-Smith and my dear friend Richard Fung. Edmund Attong captured the still images published in this book. Sonja Melton Ramesar gave permission for her work to be reproduced. I am pleased to have worked with May Yao and the capable staff at Intellect and to have had the benefit of comments from an external reviewer. Finally, this project would not have been possible without the inspiring videos of Robert Yao Ramesar. I thank him for creating work which has compelled me into new ways of writing about cinema, and for making himself and the videos available to me for the writing of this book.

INTRODUCTION

For it is the peculiar character of phenomenology to analyze and conduct research into essence within the framework of a reflection that involves only pure seeing, a framework of absolute self-givenness.

– Edmund Husserl (*The Idea of Phenomenology*, 1999: 39)

Caribbeing is an aesthetic that I have been developing for both still and motion pictures since 1986. At its core, it is an attempt to represent the supernatural essence of Caribbean existence beyond the realm of linear realism imposed by colonial rationalist convention.

– Robert Yao Ramesar ("Caribbeing: Technique and Technology in Caribbean Still and Motion Picture Aesthetics," 1997: 1)

Robert Yao Ramesar's Parlour People *begins with a colourful, shimmering image. We see its form and quality more than its contents. It is a solarized image—of the kind exposed to light before it has been fully "set," giving the impression of an image coming into being, trembling with a kind of latent energy that speaks of volume, vision and depth.[1] The image is almost still, but there is a vibrational undertone that suggests a presence beyond what is given to us in appearance. The objects in the image are indistinct, but we detect a room full of boxes, jars, shelves and countertops that fill the screen. The objects seem to spill out of their containers towards us. There is a man seated at the bottom left. He is captured in long shot and is dwarfed by the scene. The title of the video appears. The next image is in black and white.*

The camera begins a slow, halting pan across a row of glass jars. It starts with a woman at far right. She wears glasses and a print dress and her hair is pulled into a bun. The movement of the camera is staccato—a broken yet continual motion. We see the jars at eye-level and close-up. In the jars lie childhood treasures—small round lollipops, soft square bubblegum, flat round sweets— and we know instinctively that they are colourful. A voice off-screen tells us that the Kassim Ali store was established in 1938. These are the confections of memory—and the staccato movements are a journey into the past. The colour returns, gradually working its way into our consciousness, bleeding into the edges of that past. The image becomes strangely familiar. Jars are now revealed to us in full and natural light. The seated man reappears. He is older. He wears glasses. The camera slowly takes him in—and we recognize. The camera continues its pan and settles on a younger man, Farzan Ali, proprietor. His is the voice of the off-screen narration. He is interviewed about the history of the community and the store. We are returned to the present day. On the wall, a calendar reads "January 1996." The scene is Dow Village, California, Trinidad and Tobago.

We move to a long shot of the building. The sun shines brilliantly. The pale green doors are open. We stay for a short while, contemplating the scene. Countertops sit on wide glass cases, stacks of goods towering above them in the background. We approach the building from the left, but we strain with the camera as it seems to push through invisible boundaries towards the store. The movement is halting, as it was before, but as we move into this image we seem to encounter resistance. The camera finally enters and surveys. The tension of the earlier movement gives way to curiosity and investigation. The camera explores the items on display—marbles in glass cases, brooms that reach the ceiling, paper bows that twirl in the wind.

The scene is shot at a low angle as though from the perspective of a child. We look on in wonder, seeing each item as if for the first time. We gaze upon them, as if each contained a mystery that could reveal something about how it came to be in the world for our vision. The camera moves in and pulls out—flitting. It meets the marbles and examines them. It seems almost to contact them, dwells for a time and briskly moves away. At first these movements seem random. Yet there is a directionality in the movement that seems to come, not merely from the camera, but from the objects themselves. It is as if these objects have put themselves on display. They present themselves to our consciousness with the intention of being seen. But they retain some secrets still; they repel the gaze of the camera before full contact is made.

We return to Farzan Ali and to the opening scene. We are introduced to Ayub Ali, uncle of Farzan, seated at the bottom left of the screen. The camera stops briefly, as if to ensure that we have captured the significance. He is the man of the solarized image. Our access to him is mediated by prior knowledge of what now seems to us to have been an intimation of his inner core—that underlying presence that spilled out towards us and now lies dormant, no longer revealed.

Parlour People is video asserting itself in relation to objects—and objects looking back. Something essential is revealed in the seeing and the video offers us contact with that experience. I feel drawn in my viewing of *Parlour People* to contemplate the image as a repository of unfolding presence. Each instance of the camera's probing reveals a sight that is not yet complete—the sight of an object that reveals itself only partially and exists beyond its mere appearance. Objects seem to have intention—to have "a mind of their own." They seem to have consciousness—and to use that consciousness as a way of calling attention to their own being-in-the-world. Objects address my consciousness in an attempt to complete their appearance in the world. They address me as part of a collective consciousness that exists beyond the frame and makes vision possible. The video facilitates the coming forward of objects' consciousness to meet our own.

I am concerned in this book with the ways in which consciousness is brought to visibility through the medium of the moving image. I am particularly interested in the contribution made by Trinidadian film-maker Robert Yao Ramesar to our understanding of that process.[2] Ramesar has developed a distinctive aesthetic—Caribbeing—through which he attempts to make visible a Caribbean reality submerged through centuries of colonialism, slavery and indenture. He seeks to jog the audience's memories of the deep past, removing the veil imposed by the colonial experience (Ramesar 1997: 1–2). Through the use of slow motion, natural light and shadow, he aims to facilitate reconnection with a collective unconscious that resonates with the existence of a Caribbean essence. It is an effort to allow Caribbean essence to manifest.

3

Parlour People is a compelling example of exploration, interrogation and vision which begins to address broader questions of essence and manifestation in Ramesar's work. The video presents a journey between past and present through a manipulation of colour and the quality of movement. It takes us on that journey by helping us to attach to the camera's probing view and to feel the call of the objects under exploration. The suspended animation of staccato motion in *Parlour People* allows us to dwell on objects but also to dwell with our experience of looking. The video presents to us our act of looking as much as it does the objects that are seen. It drains scenes of their colour and restores them anew. In this way, objects seem to be reduced to their essentials and re-presented to us for vision as a form of "pure seeing."

In Ramesar's work, attention to the object is an attempt to address both its material and non-material dimensions. The use of darkness and silhouette is intended to convey the presence of invisibles and intangibles. It is a displacement of what he terms "colonial rationalist convention" (Ramesar 1997: 1). Ramesar is interested in the colonial legacy and the residual traces that might offer a counterpoint to it. Yet his sense of Caribbean essence is not limited to nativist assertions of a pre-colonial ancestral past insulated from the interventions of culture and history. In his view, Caribbean essence is ancestral spirit rooted in the past and manifested through contemporary local histories—continually evolving, *present*, *becoming* (Ramesar 2004). It is not immediately accessible through what is now our habitual mode of seeing. The ability to truly see—beyond mere appearances and into the essence of the object itself—produces vision as an act of consciousness tied to our experience and perception of reality. I understand Caribbeing as an attempt to restore—and re-situate—a particular way of seeing as a way of being-in-the-world. Ramesar's aesthetic strategies are an attempt to create the conditions under which that way of seeing might become possible.

Ramesar has directed over fifty documentaries and two feature films. His documentary work explores traditional culture, community life and individual biographies in Trinidad and Tobago. His features are futuristic fiction. Ramesar tends to unsettle native and non-native viewers' relationships to culture by suggesting that the cultural object is given only partially in appearance. Culture and ritual are tied to essence, character and performance. We witness their transformation. He slows down the rituals and allows us to step inside. The formal techniques serve to dislodge audiences' sedimented viewing of

4

the cultural object. They allow us to see it anew. Ramesar treats culture, in a sense, as a found object. It is an artefact of the everyday that is formally manipulated and re-conceptualized to produce a new image or idea. But this is not simply an aestheticization of culture—it is a recognition of culture's aesthetic potential.

Ramesar's early writing on his work (Ramesar 1996, 1997) discusses the imperative to find appropriate technological tools and aesthetic approaches for representing Caribbean reality. The writing displays an affinity with Third Cinema theorists (e.g. Gabriel 1982, 1989) who adopt an anti-colonial and anti-imperialist discourse. This discourse implies a somewhat transparent relationship between aesthetics, technology and culture. His later emphasis on *the becoming* articulates a more nuanced view of the processes of cultural formation. It demonstrates a concern with *the now* and the ways in which being—as entity and existence—manifests (Ramesar 2004). Processes of becoming are the focus of much postcolonial scholarship which attends to questions of hybridity and the fluidity of identities (e.g. Bhabha 1994). Postcolonial film scholars and film-makers have also addressed the core question of culture   (e.g. Rony 1996 and Trinh 1991, 1992 and 1999). Yet Ramesar's work does not fit neatly into any of the better-known categories of postcolonial film. It does not seek to supplement, supplant or speak to a colonial archive. It does not explicitly address questions of identity or representation.[3] It is not located in northern "host countries" where the conditions of diaspora and exile are often most keenly felt. Ramesar's attempt at reconnecting with memory is based on a profound understanding of the continuance of memory in local contexts—of its existence beneath the surface of the everyday. Its origin is not primarily in loss but in forgetting.

Ramesar's work occupies an unusual place in the context of contemporary film and video production. The overwhelming majority of the documentary pieces have been produced for national television, yet they are experimental. In their style and in their adherence to a clearly articulated director's vision, they are art cinema. Several pieces have been exhibited at international film festivals and the work therefore moves between the intimacy of local "insider" audiences, for whom it was originally designed, and a broader "outsider" audience for whom the connection is likely to be more interesting at the level of form. This movement is important because it situates Ramesar's production at the intersection of a number of potential points of access. In the context of the American avant-garde, for example, the work resonates with that of Maya Deren in its emphasis on rhythm, ritual, the unconscious and dream. Ramesar offers dreamlike sequences in which a collective unconscious might be made accessible through rhythmic manipulations of vision. He creates poetic movements that restore us to the world and connect us to a sense of invisible yet pervasive presence. This begins to echo the descriptions of media-making in an Aboriginal community in northern Australia where the Ancestral is not disappearing but "cultural subjects are becoming unable to perceive it" (Deger 2006: 75). Media here can serve as a means of securing a reconnection. Deger draws on "phenomenologically inflected sensibilities" (Deger 2006: xxvi), though not phenomenology's methods, to address questions of mimesis and technology in a Yolngu community. Hers is a rich and insightful ethnographic account of identity, cultural production and belonging. I am interested in the *aesthetic* qualities of Ramesar's work which—while rooted in connections to the specific and the local—place it within a broader conversation related to consciousness, manifestation and the visual.

I am interested in the ways in which phenomenology as an attitude towards the world and towards our experience of it might usefully be taken up through a reflection on Ramesar's work. As a philosophical method aimed at gaining access to the essence of objects, phenomenology offers a way of understanding the impetus and the processes at work in Ramesar's videos. As a reflection on the experience of perception, phenomenology offers a framework for the description of visual experience. As a theory of being, it opens a door to manifestation and presence. I am interested in what the phenomenological attitude might have to offer in the way of facilitating a sustained engagement with the viewing experience—a means of theorizing and staying close to my original encounter with these videos as aesthetic objects. I am concerned also with the ways in which Ramesar's work itself displays a phenomenological attitude, performing its own philosophical inquiry into being and consciousness through an extraordinary exploration of the possibilities of the visual.[4]

Phenomenology's Aims and Methods

> Phenomenology: this term designates a science, a complex of
> scientific disciplines; but it also designates at the same time and above
> all a method and an attitude of thought: the specifically philosophical
> attitude of thought, the specifically philosophical method.
>
> – Edmund Husserl (*The Idea of Phenomenology*, 1999: 19)

Edmund Husserl's phenomenology is a method for moving beyond our habitual attitude towards a philosophical one. The method involves several acts of reflection upon the ways in which objects come to be for us in our consciousness. In the natural or habitual attitude, objects are perceived through layers of assumptions and beliefs about the world which obscure their essence and preclude active engagement with the ways in which they come to be *for us*. In the philosophical attitude, we are led to a discovery of the ways in which our subjective experience of objects comes to co-constitute them as objects of and for the world. The phenomenological reduction is the key tool in Husserl's phenomenological method. It involves a leading back from the objects as they are given to us in appearance towards an inner core. It is a movement inward.

The phenomenological attitude recognizes the subjectivity of all experience and seeks to make that experience the focus of an investigation. In Husserl's investigation, this involves an appreciation of the fundamental role of consciousness in our perception of the world. For Husserl, all objects are essentially referred to consciousness or to those acts of consciousness through which objects present themselves in perception. The task of constitutive phenomenology—a phenomenology which recognizes the role of subjective experience in co-constituting objects in the world—is to analyze descriptively those acts of consciousness through which the object presents itself. The phenomenological reduction aims, through a bracketing or suspension of the world, to reflect on the acts of consciousness which bring the object into the world for us. It aims to get at our purely subjective experience of the phenomenon stripped of the vision imposed on the experience through external prejudices and assumptions. In this way, we aim to get at the "pure phenomenon"—at "the thing itself" as it exists for us—in an act of "pure seeing."

7

Ramesar's slow motion videos offer up a suspended animation within which our habitual mode of looking at the world is bracketed and new vision emerges. The camera investigates and interrogates the objects before it, searching for access to their essence. Ramesar's objects are the everyday objects of material culture and human bodies enacting the rituals of religion, history and memory. His aesthetic strategies are attempts to peel back the layers of colonial ways of looking attached to external (and internalized) assumptions about the material and the non-material world and what it is possible to perceive. Caribbeing makes the familiar strange, forcing us out of what Husserl would call our sedimented ways of viewing. In Ramesar's work, we are encouraged to adopt Husserl's philosophical attitude in our movement towards "pure seeing." It is an act that attempts to bring us closer to the objects as they come to be constituted for us in consciousness. I am suggesting that the videos themselves *perform* a phenomenological reduction which facilitates this process.

The phenomenology of Martin Heidegger can also be seen at work in Ramesar's videos. Husserl and Heidegger are both interested in that which exists beyond appearances, but their methods and emphases differ. Heidegger is concerned with notions of concealment and unconcealment and with allowing the things to "show themselves." His interest lies not in the probing investigation or reference to consciousness that we find in Husserl, but in the condition of openness that allows Being to come forward and make itself known. Husserl's phenomenology is concerned with epistemological questions about the possibility of knowledge, while Heidegger's phenomenology is concerned with the ontology of Being or existence.[5] Lovitt (1977) suggests that subjectivity, in Heidegger, is a form of receptivity to the world. Ramesar's work is grounded in an understanding of an underlying presence, and he strives to create the conditions of possibility for its appearance and for our reception of it. In his videos, the suspension performed by the phenomenological reduction opens a space into which essence and the nature of Being might be revealed.

Heidegger's phenomenology allows us to thematize the question of the intangible and presence in Ramesar's work. In Heidegger, there is a distinction between beings, being and Being. As Young (2002) outlines it, individual *beings* (human and non-human) present themselves to us in the everyday. They are the material objects that appear to us. The *essence* of those beings is what we might refer to as *being*, which *is* presence. This essence does not, itself, "presence." Finally, the generative ground of *being* or presence—that from which it

8

springs—is *Being*. Ramesar's focus on the material and the non-material implies the coexistence of these levels. Caribbeing is an attempt to create what Heidegger might call a "way of access" to them, preparing the viewer for the Dasein—or "openness-for-Being"—in which we allow the object to truly present itself to us.[6]

Husserl's phenomenology might be viewed as a movement towards, Heidegger's as a dwelling with. Phenomenological seeing requires that we *attend* to phenomena and typically that we move from the phenomena more deeply towards an inner core. Merleau-Ponty's existential phenomenology instead reaches out to the world. He focuses on perception as an embodied, enworlded experience. He dwells with experience as it is lived in and through the human body. While there is room in Merleau-Ponty's phenomenology for consciousness, this consciousness is grounded in the body and not subordinate to it. Consciousness moves through the body into the world. The body is inherently sensible because it is sensual. Perception is inherently logical and organized. The essence of things to which Merleau-Ponty gains access is attained through a heightened awareness of sensory perception and a keen receptivity to the consciousness of other beings in the world. This awareness and receptivity also gives rise to eloquent and tangible description.

> Thus when the seer is caught up in what he sees, it is still himself he sees: there is a fundamental narcissism of all vision. And thus, for the same reason, the vision he exercises, he also undergoes from the things, such that, as many painters have said, I feel myself looked at by the things, my activity is equally passivity— which is the second and more profound sense of narcissism: not to see in the outside, as others see it, the contour of a body one inhabits, but especially to be seen by the outside, to exist within it, to emigrate into it, to be seduced, captivated, alienated by the phantom, so that the seer and the visible reciprocate one another and we no longer know which sees and which is seen. (Merleau-Ponty 1968: 139)

Objects come into visual organization for us and for themselves through a reciprocal act of looking. But reciprocity implies that vision is not necessarily attained through the sheer force of our own will. Like Husserl, Merleau-Ponty suggests that objects of vision are co-constituted by subject and object, and he is also concerned with interrogation and investigation of that object. Yet Husserl's reduction is a product of our own mental activity. For Merleau-Ponty, the object responds. Receptivity to other beings brings Merleau-Ponty's thinking closer to the work of Heidegger, but in receptivity there remains a level of work involved in getting to the thing itself. For Merleau-Ponty, vision is enabled by a certain *distance* between the seer and the thing. This distance constitutes the medium of access to vision. It is the screen through which vision becomes possible—an apt metaphor for the ways in which we experience vision in video and in Ramesar's videos in particular. In Merleau-Ponty, we palpate the object with our look—envelop it with the flesh of our gaze. This embodied gaze is met with a return look of the object. There is reciprocity of vision.

Phenomenology's Material Presence

Phenomenology's Material Presence is an attempt to reflect upon the contribution that the moving image might make to the project of philosophy and the visual. It is also an attempt to operationalize phenomenological method by making explicit the connection between the phenomenological project and video's own project of bringing to visibility. Contemporary scholars of film and phenomenology have sought to understand the kind of object that cinema is and the kind of object that cinema produces for our vision. I am driven, in part, by similar impulses. Beyond this, however, I feel compelled to take into account—and to take as the *only* account—the possibilities that Ramesar's work offers for extending the phenomenological project. I understand the phenomenological project to be one which aims to *re-cognize* the objects of the world as objects given to us and constituted for us through our subjective experience. I understand the project also to be concerned with *re-cognizing* the sense of the intangible that undergirds the objects' appearance.

Where other scholars have focused on the approaches of individual philosophers—privileging embodiment over consciousness or the immanent over the transcendental—I am guided by the rich and complex performance of the videos themselves. Ramesar's videos offer a unique opportunity for bringing several phenomenological thinkers into conversation. They provide a space for contemplating the overlapping aims and strategies not only of phenomenology and experimental cinema but of the key philosophers themselves. The experience of *encounter* occasioned by these videos suggests an aesthetic object which conducts its own investigation of the world and gathers the strategies appropriate for its use. While the work facilitates comparison with phenomenological thinking, it does not passively submit to it. Instead, the videos present themselves to us as embodied material objects capable of expressing and enacting their own consciousness in the world.

Vivian Sobchack's (1992) groundbreaking interpretation of film and phenomenology provides the basis for much of my thinking in this regard. Sobchack makes a case for the materiality of film as central to its way of being-in-the-world and to our experience of it. In Sobchack's account, the film-viewing experience involves the bodies of film-maker, spectator and film itself. She suggests that film's body *enables* the perception and expression experienced by film-maker and spectator. The film's act of seeing is presented to us and the film is "taken up by us as perception turned literally inside out and toward us as expression" (Sobchack 1992: 12). This is seeing made visible. What we experience in looking at a film is an expression of visual perception rather than merely a recorded event.

> The film experience not only *represents* and reflects upon the prior direct perceptual experience of the filmmaker *by means* of the modes and structures of direct and reflective perceptual experience, but also *presents* the direct and reflective experience of a perceptual and expressive existence *as* the film. (Sobchack 1992: 9)

In the context of *Phenomenology's Material Presence*, I have taken up this notion of the film-viewing experience as one which might incorporate the world of video and the moving image more generally.

While there is an argument to be made for medium specificity, I am suggesting that video's body in fact allows for the type of perceptive/expressive experience described here. As an instrument of mediation, it too serves as an interface between the bodies of artist and viewer, making a material connection which brings towards us a specific, embodied perception of the world. Ramesar's videos present to us acts of perception and reflection that are crucial to the phenomenological method. In this work, video's intending consciousness probes the object and expresses that investigation as a way of being-in-the-world. By attachment to the camera's movement experienced as the video's own kinaesthetic engagement with the world, we are drawn in. As the video releases movement to contemplate a scene, our consciousness expands to dwell with that image. Video's peculiar characteristics of intimacy and immediacy secure the attachment more fully. In Ramesar's work, video does not merely *address* questions of philosophy—it *enacts* philosophical method as its own exploration of the world. Video's material body makes that possible.

This book is divided into three principal chapters, each exploring one of Ramesar's videos in relation to phenomenological method. I have chosen *Heritage: A Wedding in Moriah, Mami Wata* and *Journey to Ganga Mai.*[7] These videos each deal with ritual and lend themselves easily to an experience of visual encounter in the context of memory and forgetting. They are among Ramesar's most experimental pieces and open themselves—and us—to the possibility of phenomenological seeing. The first is a Christian wedding of yore, re-enacted as public performance. The second and third are religious ceremonies—Orisha and Hindu respectively—that are currently practised. In Chapter 1, I introduce the three stages of Husserl's phenomenological reduction. I suggest that *Heritage: A Wedding in Moriah* employs the methods of the psychological reduction—distancing and reflection—encouraging the movement of consciousness and inviting the viewer into an experience of memory. Chapter 2 elaborates on the eidetic and transcendental reductions to show the effects of Merleau-Ponty's "concretion of visibility" and Heidegger's manifestation of being in *Mami Wata*. In Chapter 3, *Journey to Ganga Mai* is put forward as the culmination of the phenomenological enquiry. There I describe the strategies through which *Journey* draws us fully into the space of the video and towards a mystical experience of contact and immersion. In the Conclusion, I revisit the question of phenomenological intention and suggest ways in which these videos might extend and enhance our interpretation of the cinema-viewing experience.

I have written this book with a keen sense of responsibility towards the video objects and towards my experience of them. In keeping with Husserl's phenomenological method, I have sought to reflect on the acts of consciousness which make my viewing possible. I provide close descriptions of the videos and bracket the non-essentials in an effort to minimize the distractions. In telling, reworking and reiterating, I attempt to stay close to the performance of the videos and to their intention—and to the performance of my own reflection.

This is the method of the reduction. It must continually be repeated. But I attempt also to write *into* the videos rather than around them in an effort to maintain some level of contact, however ephemeral, with my initial encounters. This is a journey intended to replicate in some measure the phenomenological registers of experience as mediated through video.

Stills from *Heritage: A Wedding in Moriah*. Courtesy the artist.

Chapter 1
Acts of Consciousness

All questions of existence and reality are bracketed in the phenomenological reduction. That they are bracketed does, however, not mean that they are gone. They are there, but we are no longer asking what is real and what is not real. Instead we ask: What is involved in being real? What are the structures of consciousness thanks to which we experience something as real? And how do they differ from the structures of our consciousness when we experience something as dream or phantasy?

– Dagfinn Føllesdal ("The Thetic Role of
Consciousness," 2003: 11–12)

Heritage: A Wedding in Moriah *begins with towering figures in top hats and coats. They carry large umbrellas and move across our field of vision against a startling "yellow" sun. We look up to them—and to the sun—from ground level. The image is in sepia and moves in slow motion. There is the music of fiddles and drums. The first title comes on-screen and is followed by blackout. The next scene is of a procession of couples also in fancy dress. They seem to skip lightly along the road. Their clothes have movement. The subtitle appears and we re-enter the black. Next we see musicians—mostly seated on the ground—providing a visual for the sound. We look up to the trees. A man emerges from a car. We see an older woman walking towards a large open gate. We see her from behind. The image blacks out. A group of men appears, again in coattails and hats.*

Again there is the sun and the figures truly stand out. They consume the screen. There is more black—and a man and woman appear. The camera focuses on the folds of a dress—pleats and puckers and stark whiteness. It examines one area of the dress and moves up to women's faces. They are awash in "white." Cut to black. We move in with the camera in slow, halting motion to a necklace on a young woman's neck. The pearls seem almost to call to us and we zoom in tentatively yet with purpose. The young woman's dress is light in colour. She turns and we see her in profile. She is smiling. It is as if she knows we have been watching, although she does not look at us directly. It is the first time that we feel acknowledged. We have approached her at eye-level. We see her face against a backdrop of others—almost layered—and against the light. We see depth. The music continues.

Cut to black. We linger on the faces of young children and zoom out. We are in the scene. We black out—out of consciousness? When we return we are in the midst of the dress we have seen earlier, and this time we move up to a hand holding a bouquet. The woman presents a sharp silhouette against trees and sunlit sky (we see her in profile) even though her dress is light in colour. How is it that we see contrast when there is so little darkness there? We next see a man smoking a pipe; his face in exquisite fullness stares directly at us. He wears an earring. He is the top layer in a series of faces. He comes out at us although he remains in the frame. His fullness occupies it. The camera approaches and recedes thickly, as if through a veil. The image seems to disintegrate in the process. We move on to other characters in this wedding procession, many dancing as they walk, this time with more close-ups and more shots at eye-level. There is no narrative order here—or none that we can discern. We see in long shot also and there is now distance and closeness. The music diminishes and a woman's voice penetrates the soundscape. She is a heckler commenting on the wedding. We do not see her. We see the bride, her father and the bridal party making their way along the road. The visual tone has changed. The colour is almost black and white. The building we see is stone—maybe it is the church. And we move inside—of that building? And we look over women's hats as they sit in church. Back outside there are drums being heated and tuned over fire, then the shadow of a figure on the road. Cut to black. The procession continues and we recognize faces. The voice of the woman continues. As the murmurs of the church crowd intervene (they are muffled, we can tell that they are inside the church), softening the sound, the procession seems to dissolve. We see the mass movement of people from above and then return to the street. Spectators have joined in or move along its outskirts. More black, more movement. An older man drums almost ecstatically, hitting the skin of the drum against the heel of his hand. The camera takes us back to fire and drums being tuned. Long shots, close-ups, shots from way below. Blackness. Spectators. Umbrellas and a brilliant sun. The procession continues its slow motion. An elderly woman inadvertently finds herself at the centre of our view. She is facing us. Credits begin. They punctuate the image. They do not roll.

Heritage sits somewhere between memory and dream. It presents a re-enactment of a traditional wedding at the Tobago Heritage Festival. Its characters are all acting. The ceremony is not "real." Yet I feel that I am a part of this procession, on the outside looking in and on the inside looking out. It is not that I can fully inhabit the characters' bodies or that they fully inhabit mine. It is that I have been there, in this scene, and I come forward now to meet myself looking at myself as I might have been. It is a memory of what has not been. And it is also dream. I drift in and out of scenes in no logical order. Present, past and future intermingle freely. Ramesar's *Heritage* is a re-enactment parading as memory and experienced as dream.

Performing the Reduction

Philosopher Natalie Depraz offers a deeply insightful interpretation of Husserl's phenomenological reduction by establishing the method of the reduction as a "disciplined embodied practice" (Depraz 1999: 95) and outlining the tensions surrounding objectivity and subjectivity in philosophical discourse. Depraz suggests that the co-existence of the practical/embodied/existential and theoretical dimensions is "at the heart of the very gesture of the reduction" (Depraz 1999: 96). She suggests further that reflection and incarnation, contemplation and action cross-fertilize to become eventually indistinguishable one from another. Depraz is concerned with elucidating the strategies at work in three reductions—the psychological, the transcendental and the eidetic. The psychological reduction involves disengagement and a subsequent "freeing up" of experience. I free myself from the object in order to take cognizance of the act of consciousness which is directed towards it. This stepping back is not a removal from the world or from the reality of the object but a leading back to experience and an enlarging and intensifying of experience that frees me from the pre-givenness of the world. The psychological reduction must be made and remade as the subject repeatedly becomes re-immersed in the worldliness of the object. There is a temporal lag between the return to the act of consciousness (or perceptual act) and the experience of perception itself. The return to the perceptual act is situated "in the aftermath of the perception of the object" (Depraz 1999: 98). This is the same for the immediate past (the past retentionally held in mind) and the present remembering of a past situation.

Heritage presents a series of retentional acts as the present remembering of a past situation and slows motion to allow for probing or exploration. *Heritage* holds the procession of characters in suspension so that we might free ourselves from the objects *per se* and spend time on the act of perceiving them. This reflection is always a recapitulation—"the two perceptual registers (object/act)" are not contemporaneous (Depraz 1999: 99). The reflection on the act of perception is therefore inherently fragile and Depraz interprets Husserl's introduction of the *epoché*—in the transcendental reduction—as an effort to confer stability on the process. *Epoché*, in Depraz's formulation, corresponds to a "gesture of suspension with regard to the habitual course of one's thoughts, brought about by an interruption of their continuous flowing" (Depraz 1999: 99). In this view, it is the mundane thought—the thought tied to the perceived object in the world and to it alone—that turns the subject away from the observation of the perceptual act. And it is the thought, rather than the world, that is bracketed. The *epoché* is not negation. The thought ceases to be relevant to the investigation.

> In this way, I enlarge my field of experience by intensifying it, by allowing another dimension to emerge from it, a dimension which precisely frees me from the ordinary pre-givenness of the world…I learn to look at the world in another way, not that the first is negated or even radically altered in its being, nor that certain objects are henceforward substituted for others but, from the simple fact that my manner of perceiving, my visual disposition, has changed, objects are going to be given to me in another light. (Depraz 1999: 98)

This is the context within which *Heritage* might be interpreted. The object before us on-screen is no longer, by virtue of Ramesar's distancing and interrogative techniques, merely itself. It becomes more than its ordinary givenness and we are able to perceive the act of consciousness which brings it to us. But this experience is transitory. We slip all too easily into the natural attitude. At every moment, says Depraz, she is caught up once again in the perceived object and must make an effort to return to the perceptual act or "the visual act in its very occurrence" (Depraz 1999: 98). There is a temporal lag always in the passage from the object to the act. *Heritage* bridges a gap between the retentional and the remembering. The retention of what has been presented to us in the video (the immediate past or near-present) is taken up by our consciousness as personal memory (a remembering) of having been a part of the procession in the world beyond the video, in the past. The shift in attention from one to the other is reflected in Ramesar's shift from long shots to close-ups.

The depth of field which we find in *Heritage* also contributes to the feeling of distance. High contrast clearly delineates all objects in the foreground. Each person exists atop the others. The sense of depth and layering is reminiscent of a stereoscopic view. A stereoscopic view presents two slightly different views of the same scene and layers them to produce the impression of a three dimensional scene, particularly of the figures in the foreground. The images in the foreground are clearly demarcated and appear to have volume. The stereoscopic view gives the observer the sense of having "been there," but the images do not move towards the viewer as do the characters of *Heritage*. The raised quality of the image—the "lifting" quality in Ramesar's video—brings an air of texture. Yet it also creates space. In the stereoscopic view, the space is real—it is a result of the placing together of slightly different views. In *Heritage*, the illusion of space comes from the gap created by the movement of consciousness between the object of perception and the reflection upon the act of perception, as well as the spaces or gaps within the image itself.[8] The gaps within the image allow an entry point for our own physicality and consciousness. They also allow the illusion of distance between the characters and their background—this is a function both of backlighting and of shooting directly into the sun, in keeping with Ramesar's vision for Caribbeing. The edges of the characters stand as an indication of a gap between foreground and background, and this conceptually allows the experience and impression of space. Behind the characters and before the background is a field.

Stills from *Heritage: A Wedding in Moriah*. Courtesy the artist.

Ramesar has indicated that one of his techniques is aimed at a type of "bastardization" of the still and moving image and between film and video (Ramesar 2004). *Heritage* appears to lift the characters out of print and guide them towards a holding cell of consciousness. In essence, the characters seem to come to life in a liminal space between a photographic past and the viewer's filmic present. The characters in *Heritage* seem to exist in photographs of the past moving towards us in the present. Images in photographs exist in a deathlike state. The characters in *Heritage* call us in to witness and experience that limbo between life and death, sleep and wake, dream and wakeful consciousness. We search them for memories, we search them for clues, and when they transform themselves into memory they hover forever at the edge of consciousness. We enter and are transformed in our looking. This space is in fact a space between movements. As a consequence of this "lifting," we proceed to an expansion of consciousness.

Depraz's temporal lag affords us an opportunity to contemplate that which is created in between spaces. The temporal lag allows us to think about the gaps in *Heritage* as the distance between perception itself and consciousness of the perceptual act. It allows us to see that consciousness as able to insert itself into the gaps. It allows us to imagine that the consciousness of the characters and the consciousness of the viewer meet in that space and commingle—and that in this commingling, the consciousness of the viewer is invited to attend to the physicality of the character by entering the character's space of the frame. Once we return to perception itself we are there, in the frame, on the screen and in the body (not our own). And that link that we feel—the trace that connects our present body outside of the frame (our viewing body) with our body that acts within the frame—is the thread that holds together the act and reflection upon the act.

In *Heritage*, Ramesar plays with low angles and eye-level shots in ways that reinforce a movement back and forth between childhood and adult memory, past and near-present. Only the children are shot at eye-level at the beginning of the tape, reinforcing the notion that a child's perspective is at play. The camera hovers around the swirls of ladies' skirts and moves up to capture the faces of the owners bathed in washes of light. The effect is almost one of revelation as the towering figures stand against the washes. A combination of close-ups and long shots gives the sense of distance and immersion. Shadows and high contrast provide detail and volume. We are invited to look—the details are offered up.

The camera draws us towards faces—there is intimacy and familiarity. We are asked to pay attention here—to capture, lock onto, engage. We are removed from the perspective of childhood to an attitude of the present by the insertion of voice. It is as if the video's characters intend that we should shift perspective. It is not the camera which intends but the characters themselves through direct looking/gazing and engagement with the camera. The entire video is dreamlike while, at the same time, its sepia tones evoke a sense of history. It is a series of photographs come to life—staccato movements halting across a surface—dandies and ladies stepping out of early twentieth century photography and into consciousness.

Memory and Dream

Cinema concentrates the experience of time and so enhances experience, makes it significantly longer, more invested, more typical, more memorable. This diffusion of idea and feeling into time is nothing much to do with screentime, with the clock time of the image on the screen. It is to do with duration, the experience of time, a kind of memory happening now.

– Susan Dermody ("The Pressure of the Unconscious upon the Image: The Subjective Voice in Documentary," 1995: 303)

Susan Dermody (1995) has written of the dream state induced by a form of associative rhythm in film. In these films, there is a sense of ritual which invokes drama but subsequently leaves drama for dream. Dermody's claim is suggestive since it causes us to think about the role of time in the experience of memory. *Heritage* meanders in the way that dreams often do. We have the impression of snatches of personal memory from which our dreams are drawn. The disembodied voices of woman and priest serve to further heighten this sense of a dream-space, within which sensory information may come to us from anywhere and is incorporated into the general feeling of "being there." We flit about from middle to beginning to end as is our wont in the dream state. Dermody is influenced by the writing of film-maker Andrei Tarkovsky. Tarkovsky writes that people go to the cinema for "time lost or spent or not yet had" (Tarkovsky 1987: 63). Although his critique of poetic cinema in the same volume does not appear to support the underlying impulses of Ramesar's work, his insight into the experience of time within film is helpful. According to Tarkovsky, the cinema image comes into being during shooting. Editing creates film's structure but not its rhythm. Film's rhythm is inherent in the image. In this view, Ramesar's *Heritage* would seem to be a work of time created in each shot. Yet the slow motion that is the most enduring characteristic of the work is introduced in the editing. It gives the characters their halting motion—and the camera its tentative gesture—and it is produced after the fact. How can we account for the experience of flow and discontinuity—of memory and dream?

Tarkovsky is not wrong to suggest that time and rhythm inhere in the image at the time of shooting. The *trace* of the time of the original event may be transferred to the film and thus inhere in the image. Marks (2002) has suggested that both analogue and digital video bear indexical traces of the events they record. If this is the case, and if time is an inherent part of the organization of an event—of the organization of an object *as* an object and an event *as* an event— then I would suggest that something essential about the time of the event may be captured in the shooting and conveyed to us as the tape. Editing can help us to tap into a particular configuration of time that organizes the original and transforms the video into an experience of time that seems somehow "proper" to the event. The young woman with the pearl necklace turns slowly towards us and away from a group of others. The man with the pipe stares directly at us and does not move. It is difficult to imagine them moving or standing still at any other speed. Stillness and motion convey a sense of time. The blackouts that punctuate my experience of time, making vision discontinuous, also give the video its rhythm. The blackouts, paradoxically, also contribute to the flow or stream of consciousness. They develop their own pattern and rhythm and are expressive in their own right. Events in *Heritage* do not unfold in linear fashion. Yet from the towering figures, to the procession, to the man exiting the car, to the details of the dress there is an association of rhythm—a rhythm enhanced by the looped phrases of fiddle and drum.

In *Heritage* there is no commentary and the voices which we hear are disembodied. We are left to our own interpretation. We see the musicians in the procession, beside the procession, playing and tuning instruments. And then, there is a voice. The eruption of a woman's voice into the consistently undulating rhythm of Tobago fiddles draws the viewer into a new relationship with the screen. The bride and her party approach the hall in which the wedding will be held. Her train is carried by an attendant. The camera is at the eye-level of the adults and from a distance the procession can now be experienced as a series of staccato movements—micromovements—that glide haltingly across the screen. A drama is unfolding. The screen literally acts as a stage across which the performers move. The action seems now to begin with the voice of the woman editorializing at the scene. The woman comments loudly on the action and questions the motives of the bride and groom as well as the groom's fidelity. She suggests that the groom has fathered a number of children out of wedlock. It is a ritual sparring with only one partner. The voice of the priest is heard to intone the virtues of marriage and the crowd is heard to respond with laughter to the commentator's barbs. The priest eventually responds with restraint. The disembodied voices contribute to our dreamlike experience. We are returned to the present of the event.

The procession has been leading into a church and a larger cast of characters has joined the ensemble. A woman carrying a chest stands out. The commentator's voice continues—as does that of the priest. Meanwhile, the camera has returned to the scene outside, to couples walking side by side, pairs of elegantly dressed guests, the men's umbrellas shading them both. And the couples seem to prance, to jump, to saunter in slow motion. The women's dresses billow—they have volume and depth. The men's legs are caught in the elemental motions of being outstretched. They move towards the viewer but off to the left. They seem to be heading towards us but are not interested in us at all. And there is a disjuncture between the sound and the image. Prior to the eruption of voice, we imagine the music simply as diegetic sound run as a loop over the visual scene. Here we are forced to recognize separation, and the dreamlike quality is enhanced. There is a more forceful rupture between image and sound. The result is further disembodiment.

Theorist Michel Chion (2000) has suggested that sound can influence the perception of time in an image in three significant ways—through temporal animation, temporal linearization or vectorization. In my reading of Chion, temporal animation literally allows us to perceive time as moving. In temporal linearization, we are encouraged to perceive a beginning, middle and end of action and this contributes to our impression of causality. Vectorization suggests movement of the image, narrative or action towards the future. In each instance, sound positions the image temporally—providing an aural context within which to comprehend the image and allowing us to anchor the image in time. In order to lend itself to being influenced temporally, the image must be static or have partial movement of its own. Ramesar's work is replete with microrhythms which contribute to the influence of sound on our perception of time. According to Chion, visual microrhythms are "rapid movements on the image's surface caused by things such as curls of smoke, rain, snowflakes, undulations of the rippled surface of a lake, dunes, and so forth—even the swarming movement of photographic grain itself, when visible" (Chion 2000: 119). Microrhythms create "rapid and fluid rhythmic values, instilling a vibrating, trembling temporality in the image itself" (Chion 2000: 119). In *Heritage*, microrhythms and slow motion combine to create a sense of "trembling temporality."

Chion suggests that sound is more quickly perceived than image. We are more quickly attuned to sound, which comes to us through time, than the visual, which comes to us through space. According to Chion, sound implies movement. If movement is also about time, then this would help to explain why I see the characters moving towards me in ways that elongate the experience of time. Time and movement are stretched out and we insert ourselves into the gaps. The added value of the sound is, in the case of the music, to animate the characters even further by transforming vibrating temporality into a form of potential movement. There is an element in the sound that plays at the edges of the characters in the image—a type of concordance that gives them fullness. At the moment when we hear voices off-screen, that particular experience of temporality is broken and replaced by an experience of vectorization. The characters are returned to memory as a loop but they move towards a future also. The grain of the video gives the impression of depixellation—of disintegration of the image. The image appears to be subtly breaking down into its elemental parts—showing us what it is made of and creating further gaps and spaces for entry. We enter the scene to join the characters as they journey towards us through time.

The clarity of the voices juxtaposed with the dreamlike quality of the image produces an evenness of tone and further distance between us and the scene. The voices jolt us out of our journeying through time to return to a present sensation. This time, we are in a present happening now, to rework Dermody's phrase. Image and sound work together such that the clarity of the heckler's voice closes a gap—and with that gap, the relationship between consciousness of character and consciousness of viewer is temporarily closed. We go back to seeing these characters as a cast across a screen. We recognize their faces and we are returned to the familiar with something added—the shift effected through the psychological reduction has brought us to perception anew. The sound closes the zone of commingling and brings us abruptly out of suspension. The sound and image are no longer seamless and this exposure of difference seals the gap. It interrupts the flow of consciousness and the procession continues—this time without further insertion. We observe as if we are present at a wedding happening now but we see the scene quite differently.

Movement, Memory and Consciousness

> Memory, inseparable in practice from perception, imports the past into the present, contracts into a single intuition many moments of duration, and thus by a two[-]fold operation compels us, de facto, to perceive matter in ourselves, whereas we, de jure, perceive matter within matter.
>
> – Henri Bergson (*Matter and Memory*, 1988: 73)

In *Matter and Memory*, Henri Bergson addresses the problem of matter, consciousness and their relation. He does this as a way of avoiding the dichotomy between subjective idealism and materialistic realism. One of Bergson's key insights is the notion that matter and consciousness—and the related phenomena of pure perception and memory—differ not only in intensity but also in nature. Pure perception occupies a certain depth of duration whereas subsequent "perceptions"—or memories—are not real moments of things but moments of our consciousness. *Heritage*, by altering our experience of duration, draws the viewer simultaneously into an experience of pure perception and an experience of consciousness. *Heritage* offers up "pure perception" as moments of our consciousness. Each interrogation and exploration of the camera is taken up by us as a "subsequent perception" by virtue of the fact that we have inserted ourselves into the gaps in the image and taken on the experience of memory. *Heritage* is taken up as an act of pure recollection founded on a moment and

26

subsequent moments of perception. If memory imports the past into the present, then Ramesar's images of wedding characters are imported into the present of the viewer and that liminal space that exists between the characters themselves and the viewers. They are Bergson's survival of past images coming forward to meet and to complete the perception of the present.

Sobchack proposes that a phenomenological model of cinematic identification might differentiate among "a variety of subjective spectatorial modes that co-constitutes the cinematic object as the kind of cinematic object it is" (Sobchack 1999: 241). Sobchack also suggests that our personal and embodied existence and knowledge position our consciousness in particular ways and affect how we will take up what is given to us on the screen (Sobchack 1999: 242). She uses the work of Jean-Pierre Meunier (1969) to elaborate on identification in three types of film. According to Meunier, we take up images as existentially and specifically known to us. The *film-souvenir* or home movie is the most known, the documentary partially known and the fiction film unknown. Since the images on-screen in a fiction film are the least known to us in their specificity (they are imaginary), we are most dependent on the screen here for specific knowledge of what we see. In the *film-souvenir* we are least dependent on the screen. In this framework, the more dependent we are on the screen for knowledge, the more attention we pay to the screen, focusing our attention on, rather than through, the screen. We are less likely to work with the image to co-constitute what we see on the screen. According to Sobchack, in the *film-souvenir*, consciousness is engaged in highly constitutive activity, intending towards general recovery of the memory of a whole person or event rather than the apprehension of a specific film image. *Heritage* operates at the edge of *film-souvenir* and documentary, engaging the "native viewer" at the level of cultural familial ties but moving beyond this assumption to create memories of an event where no original event exists in the viewer's actual past.

Where Sobchack suggests a move towards the general recovery of memory in the *film-souvenir*, with Meunier I suggest an evocation of memory, a sleight of cinematic hand that tricks consciousness into producing an act of remembering.

> For Meunier, the structure of identification in the home-movie attitude is essentially one of *evocation*. That is, the function of the *film-souvenir* for its viewer is incantatory and procurative, and its images taken up as an intermediary, mnemonic, and channeling

> device *through* which the viewer evokes and identifies not with the mimetic image, but with an absent person or past event. As suggested earlier, this means that the spectator's identification with—and of—the *film-souvenir* consists essentially of subjectively mobilizing intuitive, synthetic, and personal knowledge of the viewed person or event in a *constitutive actualization* enabled by the objectively specific images on the screen…. (Sobchack 1999: 247)

Sobchack goes on to suggest that the objectively subjective images are subjectively generalized by the spectator in an always failed effort to evoke presence. The images in the *film-souvenir* are apprehended as a catalyst to a "constitutive and generalizing activity that transcends their specificity" in an effort to call up this absent whole or real person or event (Sobchack 1999: 247). Where Sobchack sees an attempt to evoke presence, *Heritage* presents the viewer with the option of entering the scene of the wedding to meet the characters and participate in the actualization of memory. The characters in this drama present themselves rather than wait for the viewer to call them into presence. They then invite the viewer in—in much the same way that Merleau-Ponty describes the calling of objects to the viewer and the reciprocal creation or establishment of vision. The *film-souvenir*/documentary experience that is *Heritage* features images that themselves call up presence and open spaces through which the viewer can add knowledge in an act of co-constitution. The video exhibits longitudinal consciousness, moving backward and forward through time.

In *Heritage*, the knowledge that is mobilized is intuitive and synthetic, but it is not truly personal. Ramesar has created the circumstances within which we might experience the work as personal memory, although it is not. There is, however, the constitutive actualization of which Sobchack speaks. It is enabled by the objectively specific images on the screen. The images on the screen are constituted by us through vision at the same time that, as viewers, we are constituted by them. We enable the characters to progress towards actualization by lending our bodies. The actualization is never complete—this is the condition of the characters' existence. The possibility of actualization is constrained by the reality of the absence of these characters in our remembering. They exist in retention and are converted into a false remembering. The retentions are stretched out and made to take up space yet true memory, as Bergson reminds us, takes place in and occupies time rather than space. This is because true memory is linked to duration—to our experience of time rather than our measurement of it.

As Sobchack has suggested, we see through the screen to some events or persons beyond it. However, we also focus on the screen, wondering at the details of the dresses and faces, drawn into the experience of perception as if for the first time. We are learning to see. Yet this focus might also be described as a focus through the objects or characters themselves. Sobchack's reading is a reading of loss—of absent people and events whose memories are triggered by the present perception of them on the screen. Their reality can never be actualized. People and events are lost to us in that particular recorded moment forever. They cannot be recuperated into the present. Yet Ramesar's video allows us to do precisely this. My interpretation is of immersion and gain rather than loss. We insert ourselves into the narrative for the first time and incorporate—and are incorporated—as though we were familiars. Our identification is tied to a present enactment of the past. We experience the work as memory and dream and are therefore called in as if to a familiar scene. The characters take this opportunity to exercise their desire to actualize in the present. And to do this they utilize our bodies.

This appropriation of the body leads to an experience of immersion. The distance which we experience through the gaps in motion (and the punctuation of blackouts) together with the gaps in the depixellated image leads paradoxically to an experience of immersion. *Heritage* evokes a memory that is not properly ours and allows us then to experience that memory in the present—Dermody's "memory happening now." And yet the characters in the video cannot ever fully actualize—they cannot leave the frame. They remind us that memory, as Bergson suggests, once actualized becomes something else entirely. The wedding characters exist, therefore, always on the cusp of realization or actualization. As living memory, they journey forward to meet and complete our present perception and find a space of congress. In that congress, our bodies are enlisted in a re-enactment. We no longer merely sit on the outside. Our bodies enter the frame to meet the characters. We enter their bodies and provide them with a physical life which they would otherwise not have. It is not the case that the characters do not possess life on the screen. It is that that quality of life has no other point of access to our present world. When we watch the procession, we watch ourselves and that is because we exist in those bodies. And so memory is able to act as though it is ours, exists in the past and comes towards our present. And so it is able also to act as though it were a dream with snatches of our own past, cut and pasted and patched together to create a narrative which bears a relation to our past without our actually having been there.

Bergson's call to recognize the *movement* that is memory—the process through which memory is called by and inserts itself into the present—is crucial to developing a framework within which to understand the call of the characters in *Heritage*. It is also fundamental to our understanding of the experience of memory as it relates to structures of consciousness explored phenomenologically. Sobchack's reading of Meunier suggests that in the *film-souvenir* we see through the film to the absent characters. In *Heritage*, we both dwell on the screen and see through it but from the other side. It is more properly the characters who are able to see through the video screen to us, and we who see imperfectly through the screen of the gaze to them. According to Bergson, memory-images are forms of attentive-recognition while spontaneous or automatic recognition (one might say immediate perception) is characterized by inattention—a form of recognition which takes us away from the object before us rather than bringing us back to dwell on it. Focus in *Heritage* is on a form of deliberate attention which is shifted primarily by the characters seeming to move away from us or invite us in rather than through any intention of our own. In this way, one might think of Husserl's focused "ray of attention" (Ihde 1973: 61) as a kind of phenomenological searching. The camera seeks out the characters, examines them from childlike and adult perspectives, focuses attention on their movements, sits fascinated by the dissolution offered by the slow motion and waits at times to see what will surface. The disjunctive audio which enters the scene as voice separates the audio and visual even further and strangely brings the viewer's attention to a midway point between attentive and automatic recognition. We already recognize the face of a man who might be an "uncle." Our attention is directed away from actual recognition and towards the creation of "new memories." In this way, the characters and the home-movie setting of the wedding provide a backdrop of familiarity against which to encounter newness.

Each character will initially be unfamiliar to us. Yet we will seek them out as objects with the potential of the familiar. We pay attention while the commentator draws us into a communal discourse—what is unfamiliar is now made to seem recognizable. Behaviour becomes familiar at the level of the body, movements and the voice. We are forced to recognize the voice of the priest since his body is unavailable to us. We must follow the discussion and so place ourselves in a position of having a ringside seat, so to speak, while not being physically present. And so we take that "perception" with us out into the street as we observe the procession once more and see by-now-familiar faces. The new bodies—the couples lined up under umbrellas, the man dancing/walking the jig—now come to present themselves as the conjuring up of the past in the present. Although the movements of the video are halting, there is fluidity in the movement of the loop that is memory and perception. What we then have is an experience of at least two currents in the work. One belongs properly to the presentation of events on-screen and the other to the presentation of memory. It is in the space between these two movements that the characters of the video realize the opportunity to step out of the work and into a holding cell of consciousness. It is there that we meet them.

The sepia tones used in *Heritage* are often associated with evocation of the past or the creation of a "period piece" in audiovisual communication. The period costumes contribute to the pull of the past into the present.[9] The pace of the video—its slow motion—also quite logically suggests a viewing that is filtered through time. The filter is made thinner—though not eradicated—by the seemingly deliberate gazes of the participants. Sobchack (1992) suggests that the film experience allows us to experience ourselves as both objects and subjects of vision. The film experience is produced by the existence, experience and expression of three bodies—the bodies of the film-maker, the film and the spectator. Like the others, film's body is a material and sensible object with intending consciousness. It is an embodied, enworlded consciousness. In Sobchack's framework, film's body performs two functions. It enables the film-maker's and the spectator's perception and expression. It is also a "*direct means of having and expressing a world*" (Sobchack 1992: 168). It is presented to us as a technologically mediated consciousness of experience and to itself as an immediate experience of consciousness (Sobchack 1992: 168). The reversibility of perception and expression suggests that what the camera perceives with its own eye is turned outward towards us as expression. We see almost as the film and camera see. In the film experience, we are looked at. It is through the actions of others—the looks of characters on-screen directed towards us and the camera—that we understand ourselves as intended objects (as objects of and for vision). What we see when we observe characters in a film looking at us is an intention that comes from outside of ourselves and reaches out towards us.

Stills from *Heritage: A Wedding in Moriah*. Courtesy the artist.

Amédée Ayfre (1969) has written that telecommunications are communication at a spatial or temporal distance. The image or voice of a person transmitted in this way is an extension of *presence* rather than a mere likeness. A recorded television event is an extension in space but also a prolonging of time. The characters in *Heritage* prolong the time of their present into ours by virtue of being *mediated* into our existence.

Merleau-Ponty (1968) offers us a way of thinking about the reciprocity of the gaze and the formation of vision. Although he is very much concerned with the immersion of the body and of consciousness in the world, he is aware of an element of distance without which immersion would not be possible. This distance is the flesh of the gaze—the thickness that constitutes our looking and the object's looking back. It surrounds the object as we palpate it with our look—intending it into vision and visibility.

> We understand then why we see the things themselves, in their places, where they are, according to their being which is indeed more than their being-perceived—and why at the same time we are separated from them by all the thickness of the look and of the body; it is that this distance is not the contrary of this proximity, it is deeply consonant with it, it is synonymous with it. It is that the thickness of the flesh between the seer and the thing is constitutive for the thing of its visibility as for the seer of his corporeity; it is not an obstacle between them, it is their means of communication. (Merleau-Ponty 1968: 135)

The thickness of the flesh is not the body of the seer or the seen but an intangible thisness that surrounds the object and acts as a transmitter or medium of vision. Mediation enables vision. There is no direct perception of the object. In *Heritage*, the thickness separating the viewer from the viewed might be thought of as a translucent veil which allows partial access from the inside and out. The veil is composed of minute pores which shift and shimmer, allowing uneven access to the objects on either side as they search for spaces or gaps in the fabric. The veil is the means of communion between viewer and viewed, enabling the intention of the viewed to reach across the video divide and invite our attention. It is the medium through which we have access to the video's world and the medium through which the video's world has access to our consciousness.

In *Heritage*, it is as if the gaze of each participant temporarily penetrates the veil and widens the access point—the pinpoint of the pinhole camera—to broaden the view for contemplation. There is the feeling of coming-into-space in the video as distance is increased and angles are widened and the camera seems to take greater control over accessing and contemplating the scene. It is the characters themselves who have allowed this access, in a sense drawing the viewer into the scene so that our bodies through our eyes follow the movements of their bodies on-screen, mimicking in stasis what their bodies perform kinetically.

> At that precise moment [when recollection, pared down, blends with perception], memory, instead of capriciously sending in and calling back its images, follows regularly, in all their details, the movements of the body. (Bergson 1988: 106)

And as we follow those movements, our bodily attitudes are predisposed to receiving gestures as though they were familiar. The deliberate staccato movements open up spaces, as though the image were again on the verge of depixellation, allowing a blanket or sheath of freed time-space moments into which the body on the outside of the scene can insert itself. Merleau-Ponty's flesh of the gaze not only brings objects into visibility but also hangs like a mesh curtain through which molecules pass freely through to one side but not the other.

According to Bergson, we must place ourselves in the past and follow and adopt the movement by which something past expands into a present image. This is precisely the process that we are invited to undergo in *Heritage*. We are called into the image the way that memory is called to meet present perception. As we enter the present of the frame we attach to the movements of the bodies which we find there. We follow the movements of the memory-body. Recollection has here blended with perception as false memories created by the video and its inhabitants out of present perception. We follow this process through to an act of quasi-materialization. We join the journey out of the photographic existence/quality into movements through space and yet we are still contained. Of what does this journey towards actualization consist? It consists of a series of identifications based on the body, invited through consciousness and manifested as/on the verge of actualization. *Heritage* invites us into the photograph (into photographic reality), uses our bodily identification and consciousness as a vehicle towards its own movement and returns us to the fabric of the veil. We do not end up where we started. Our movements are forever constrained by the endless loop that is present perception calling memory-images to join and dissipate into new structures which are no longer properly the province of memory but a new object entirely.

The sealing of the gap shuts the door on further movement towards the present. The images are not real memories. They exist at the level of dream. The photographic characters are already on the verge of movement, awaiting a body through which they can progress. The progression of bodies in this instance is also the progression of memory. This is aided in no small measure by the ritualistic, event-nature of the wedding. The characters of *Heritage* appear to have borrowed our material existence as a way of enhancing their own present. Yet their present cannot ever exist outside of the space of the screen. Memory exists in time rather than space. The journey towards the present does not traverse a physical/mental landscape but moves to various positions within the general flow of continuous time that is duration. True memory, unlike habit, is coextensive with consciousness. Our experience of the near-present is neither habit nor true memory but it is linked to the experience of the latter. Drawn into the folds of memory, invited to join the cycle that sees memory-images forever called to the present perception in order to complete that perception, we find ourselves "caught" in a process that does not in fact complete the present but repeats a simulacrum of the past.

A memory-image is actualized or materialized when it comes to the present—at which point it ceases to be a memory-image and becomes something else entirely. The characters in *Heritage* do not yet merge with present perception. They are present perception disguised as memory and, for this reason, they are unable to materialize. They must remain forever within the dream-space of the past, travelling unceasingly over the interval between the plane of action and the plane of dream (Bergson 1988: 170). Bergson suggests that there exist two different mental dispositions or degrees of tension—two tones—of mental life. An exploration of different modes of consciousness is a productive point of entry for elaborating on Bergson's theory of memory in *Heritage*. The thetic role of consciousness deals precisely with the tones of mental life.

"The Thetic Role of Consciousness"[10]

Heritage shows us that an act of remembering something that we have not experienced can be taken up by consciousness as real. Husserl makes reference to memory, in *The Idea of Phenomenology*, as a way of establishing the relationship between essence as it is given in perception and essence as it is given in our imagination. Primary memory, according to Husserl, is the retention that is necessarily bound up with every perception. The experience I now have becomes objective for me in immediate reflection. In the current experience of perception, the same object also and at the same time continues to present itself. The object retains the same tone in current perception and primary memory, moving back into the past to constitute the same objective point in time. This tone may endure and continue to present itself even though its content may change. For Husserl, this is evidence that seeing reaches beyond the "pure now-point" and is capable of intentionally holding on, in a "new now," to what no longer exists in the present (Husserl 1999: 49). The movement and re-presentation of the object allow us to think of primary memory and present perception as a loop and of primary memory, in particular, as an event that is never fully closed in the present.

Dagfinn Føllesdal (2003) provides a framework for thinking through the process by which we come to understand the presence of the characters in *Heritage* as the presence of our personal past. According to Føllesdal's reading of Husserl, consciousness is made up of the noema, the noesis and the hyle.[11] The *act* of consciousness consists of the noesis and the hyle. The noesis is the meaning-giving element of the act while the hyle are experiences we have when the sense organs are affected. Situated outside of the act, in a coordinating role, is the noema. Føllesdal refers to the noema as the meaning given in the act. It determines the temporal features of the object of the act but is not itself temporal. The noema is made up of a noematic sense and a thetic component. This thetic component allows consciousness to distinguish different kinds of acts such as those of perception, remembering and imagination (Føllesdal 2003: 11). There are several thetic components within consciousness but the one which deals with perception addresses our conceptions of reality and existence.

Føllesdal suggests that Husserl was particularly interested in the difference between acts in which we experience something as real and those in which we do not. Perception and remembering, for example, may share the same object, yet they are entirely different acts of consciousness. In attending the live event

36

of the wedding in Moriah, we may see a man in coattails in the procession and acknowledge him to be the groom. In this act of perception, the hyle play a key role and must harmonize with the noesis to produce the object (the man) for our consciousness. In *remembering* the event, the hyle we now have are typically not relevant to the act. We remember the past event—our encounter with the groom at the wedding—without seeing the groom in the present. But the present hyle are at times relevant to our remembering. Our memory of the groom might be triggered by an experience in the present that takes us back to the original moment. It is also possible that the object (the man) may have left traces for which we now look in the present—traces which may corroborate or make less plausible what we remember (Føllesdal 2003: 15). In both perception and remembering, Føllesdal suggests, our acts are constrained by our sensations or hyle and we experience the object as real.

In viewing *Heritage,* we see the man in coattails in an act of present perception—but the wedding is a re-enactment of a past event which we have not actually attended. Along with this present perception is Husserl's primary retention, returned to us repeatedly as we watch the video procession. As we enter the frame of the video through the gaps in slow motion, we take with us the retentionally held perceptions of the groom's existence. These retentions are transformed into traces which enter and re-enter the perpetual loop that is the interaction between perception and primary memory. As our consciousness meets the consciousness of the characters and is incorporated into the latter, the replaying of retentions extends into an experience of memory. In the loop that is the interaction between perception and primary memory, each retention takes us further back into the impression of an "original" moment. The thetic component of consciousness presents us with an act of remembering. Ramesar's aesthetic strategies trick the thetic component of consciousness into producing an experience of memory. The manipulation of time and motion changes the surface of the event and the hyle are themselves affected by this manipulation. The initial perceptions, re-iterated to us in primary memory, suggest to the hyle the reality of present sensations. The prolongation of time and presence provides the effect of duration. The staccato motion opens gaps, allowing us to insert ourselves into the narrative.

There is a moment in the video when the viewer seems to be specifically invited in. The young woman with the necklace turns to look almost at us. We have been observing her surreptitiously from behind. She acknowledges the gaze, smiles and laughs. Her engagement with vision encourages our own reflection on how it is that she comes to be seen by us. We see ourselves seeing her and her vision taking it in. We become subjects and objects of vision:

> The look, we said, envelops, palpates, espouses visible things. As though it were in a relation of pre-established harmony with them, as though it knew them before knowing them, it moves in its own way with its abrupt and imperious style, and yet the views taken are not desultory—I do not look at a chaos, but at things—so that finally one cannot say if it is the look or if it is the things that command. What is this prepossession of the visible, this art of interrogating it according to its own wishes, this inspired exegesis? (Merleau-Ponty 1968: 133)

We see the *Heritage* characters as if through a veil. The characters call out to us and invite us to vision and we move forward to meet them. We move through the thickness of the flesh of the gaze in order to see. Vision—or the act of vision—becomes visible as a process of movement towards.

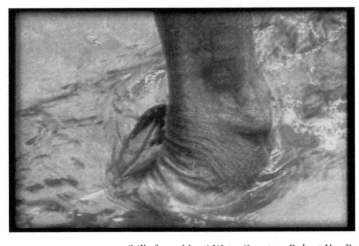

Stills from *Mami Wata*. Courtesy Robert Yao Ramesar and Sonja Melton Ramesar.

CHAPTER 2
BEING AND CONSCIOUSNESS

Being is to be laid hold of and made our theme. Being is always being of beings and accordingly it becomes accessible at first only by starting with some being. Here the phenomenological vision which does the apprehending must indeed direct itself toward a being, but it has to do so in such a way that the being of this being is thereby brought out so that it may be possible to thematize it.

– Martin Heidegger (*The Basic Problems of Phenomenology*, 1988: 21)

Mami Wata *opens with a scene of blackness. The title drops out of this blackness to reveal an underlying layer of water and fragments of movement. We next see a man seated at a drum, playing. The music is of drumming and devotional chanting. The image is in black and white and slow motion. We see the man against stark sunlight—as in* Heritage—*in the midst of a crowd. The edges of his frame seem superimposed on the people around him and almost wash out into the light of the sun. We see the scene at the eye-level of those standing. The image is full of depth and it is grainy. There is another man playing drums. We move to a man playing the* chac-chac.[12] *There is no background. The sunlight drenches the scene and absorbs all that is behind the crowd. The man moves yet we do not follow. Our camera is fixed. The crowd is a circle and we are inside. We see faces clearly. The contrast is sharp. The faces do not look at us. A priest pours libations and we see his every movement. It is dreamy and slow. In medium shot, two women begin to move at the left of the screen. They wear head-ties like most of the women in the image. They concentrate—they seem completely absorbed. The first woman begins to bend over. She rises. The other moves her arms. A man puts his hand to his forehead. He is sweating. He seems to breathe heavily. We see each of these figures clearly against the others and the background of light. The first woman is assisted by other participants.*

We move to another shot. Another woman is half-hidden to the right of the screen. She begins to move. Then we see her fully. She moves into the opening in the circle. She jumps in her dancing. The slow motion captures the movements and the contrast shows us the details of the pattern on her dress. She takes up the space of the screen. Next we see an umbrella against the sun and a man in the crowd. The woman is before us again with outstretched arms. She does not face us. Corbeaux fly overhead. The woman reaches out to another to have her head tied. She is embraced by this older woman—nestling her head in her bosom. There is softness and rigidity—their elbows stick firmly out at their sides. We see a hand in the air. The scene is dreamy. A voice punctuates the singing—"Oi!" The woman slowly turns towards us. Her eyes are large and unseeing—or all-seeing—as they look to us but past us. She sees something not visible to us at all. She moves on to embrace an older man and pours libations—oil and water— onto the ground. The camera takes us to others in the crowd—extreme contrast and no background, just white light. Two more figures are shown against the white light. We return to "our" woman—the one who has engaged us. She lifts off the ground with shoulders thrown back. The camera zooms to catch her again, this time in the distance. She moves towards us through the clearing in the circle, slowly and deliberately, as if through a veil. There is resistance that we do not see. She holds the lower portion of her dress in one hand. She concentrates. She does not see—or sees too much for us to comprehend. She moves towards us. We do not move. We are transfixed. Time—and we—stand still, but the movement continues. She almost fills and certainly exceeds the screen, her dress billowing and expanding laterally, its patterns creating volume and a staccato rhythm of their own. The crowd now forms her blurred background, but the ultimate background remains the light. The woman bows—but not to us. When we can contain her no longer, the camera transports us to another scene. The rhythm is still slow, but the pacing of the shots has quickened and we see fragments rather than wholes. The scene is of a river.[13] *The camera approaches the level of the river and does not shoot directly into the light. The contrast is lessened and the image is softer and clearer. We sense that the mood has changed although the music continues. There is a sense of almost-completion—a settling. Calabashes containing offerings float in the centre of the image, suspended. We see legs in the water, then the woman's face. She is almost fully submerged. We see a swirl of water, a foot, a calf in close-up. We see the pale heel and dark calf, the foot firmly planted in just an inch or so of water. The woman emerges to just below her shoulders. All the while, the drumming continues, linking the river scene to the one on land. She shakes her head from side to side. Her eyes are closed. She is ecstatic. We see now that this is the image underlying the title that opened the tape. We have come full circle. Where blackness covered the action we have, not light, but recognition in the form of this revealing. The woman rises. The camera returns to the foot and then to land. A bottle of olive oil and a fire are on the ground, evidence of the ceremony in which the woman has participated. We see another calabash and a fire and we rejoin the circle from a different perspective—from outside rather than within. It is as if the woman's transformative experience has altered our own relationship to the space of the event. From outside of the circle, a man walks by and looks at us. Another man walks by, in the opposite direction, from another scene. There is a long shot of water and flags along the shore. A girl wearing a* bindi *appears in a glitter of mirrors and light. The credits appear.*

Mami Wata, directed by Ramesar and Sonja Melton Ramesar, is a call to witness. It is a journey into religious possession and an injunction to dwell in the phenomenological reduction. It is principally a presentation of an Orisha ceremony interwoven with brief shots of scenes at a Hindu temple.[14] We are not invited to participate as we are in *Heritage*. We are called upon to observe. The camera does not interrogate. We stand still and watch movement unfold. What we seem to witness is the embodiment of consciousness—consciousness intending itself into the world and presenting itself to us as visible. But there is an underlying presence—the being of the participants?—that seems to come forward as well.

The "Concretion of Visibility"

Merleau-Ponty suggests that a "visible" is a kind of passage—a straits through which vision moves towards concretion. The visible is always to be understood as a point of differentiation against a background of the invisible. The visible possesses thickness, or density, but it must be fixed within its surrounding field in order to become accessible to us. A certain red, for example, is only "a certain node in the woof of the simultaneous and the successive" that is the fabric of the visible (Merleau-Ponty 1968: 132). It is "a concretion of visibility" (Merleau-Ponty 1968: 132).

> ...in general a visible, is not a chunk of absolutely hard, indivisible being...but is rather a sort of straits between exterior and interior horizons ever gaping open...a certain differentiation, an ephemeral modulation of the world—less a color or a thing, therefore, than a difference between things and colors, a momentary crystallization of colored being or of visibility. (Merleau-Ponty 1968: 132–133)

Mami Wata shows us, through possession, "a momentary crystallization" as the invisible comes to visibility.

The veil through which we move in *Heritage* is the flesh of the gaze experienced as a product and enabling factor of the mutuality of vision. It is constituted through the act of vision directed from the characters and from ourselves towards each other as we engage in a process of seeing. In *Mami Wata*, our gaze is not returned. And we do not probe the object. We are presented with the object as it unfolds into new forms of subjectivity. We look through the screen to the participants and see them coming into vision not for us but for themselves. They do not address us as individuals but send forth a mode of address. My individual consciousness does not move towards the object of my vision. It is part of a broader subjective consciousness that seems to witness an invisible made concrete. The object coming into vision lies within the participants but does not belong to them. *They* belong to it. It is the background against which they are formed.

In *Mami Wata*, my consciousness apprehends the details of a face or a dress and distances itself from these objects in order to see this apprehension. It suspends its attachment to the world beyond the scene of the present ritual and receives an oncoming movement of body and invisibility. The invisible does not suddenly enter the space. It seems somehow organic to the scene and to the persons in it. It gestures towards other participants although their response seems incomplete. It becomes concretely visible through one woman's body but seems to be a background presence from which that body springs. Its intentional character suggests to us that it is consciousness, for consciousness is always *of* something and is always directional. Yet underlying presence and manifestation are suggestive of essence—the being of individual beings and the condition of their possibility. *Mami Wata* complicates the movement between essence and consciousness and the relationship between distance and appearance.

In Depraz's (1999) model, the psychological reduction—or reflective conversion—involves concentrated perceptual activity on the part of the (viewing) subject. We look, with the camera. We interrogate the image. We search for details. We take in these details even as we attempt to separate them from their context and from ourselves to focus on the act of perceiving them. This is the experience of *Heritage*. The camera moves forward in an act of interrogation. We are invited in. We move towards the characters as they move towards us. The gaps in the video and in consciousness facilitate our reflection on the *act* of vision and *structures* of consciousness and not merely on the objects of these. The psychological reduction is inherently unstable since there is always a temporal lag between the act of perception and our apprehension of it. The transcendental reduction or *epoché* is intended to stabilize the conversion by suspending our attachment to the existence of the world and limiting the perceptual and imaginative distractions—the distractions caused by extramental and mental objects.[15] In the eidetic reduction, our attachment to the empirical world is further challenged by an acknowledgement of the infinite possibilities of the real. The real as it is presented to current perception is no longer taken for granted. The factual object presented to us is but a particular modulation in the perceptual field. In the eidetic reduction, we release our hold on this modulation—and its hold on us—in order to reflect on its possibilities. Essence is possibility—the invariant structure of the object before us which may manifest in any number of ways but manifests or actualizes now in the present incarnation. For Husserl, as Depraz points out, fact (or the factual object) is abstract. It is limited to the actualization of only one possibility. Essence is concrete. It is full of potentialities (Depraz 1999: 101). Husserl's aim in getting to "the things themselves" is to address and make contact with this field of possibilities.

Mami Wata is a video in which the link between the transcendental reduction or *epoché* and the eidetic reduction shows itself. Extreme contrast and depth heighten our perception of detail (the patterns on the dress). In *Mami Wata*, we dwell in the psychological reduction long enough and intensely enough to witness the coming into being of visual organization (Sobchack 1992: 132). The *epoché*—the suspended animation experienced as a bracketing effect—works to sustain and lengthen the moment of the reflective conversion. The fixed camera positions and dreamy black and white slow motion allow us to contemplate the act of our seeing. Into this space of reflection the *essence* of the participants is able to bring itself to visibility—to manifest. What a participant might experience as the manifestation of an externally existing divinity upon and through her body is presented to us as an essence made visible through reflection. This essence does not come through gaps in the narrative or gaps in the body of video. It comes into the space of the reflective conversion. It is because we do not move forward to meet the participants that this space is lengthened before us. We co-create, with the video, the possibility of vision through a necessary distance.

Heritage performs the work of the reflective conversion for us in order that we might enter the gap. Ramesar and Melton Ramesar are able to build upon the reflective conversion by depleting the scene of its physical background. In *Mami Wata*, there is pure light. Whereas we are able to ground ourselves in *Heritage* in a physical environment and the layers of characters both on and off the screen, in *Mami Wata* the participants are in a state of animated suspension. The stereoscopic-type views which we see in *Heritage* are exaggerated here. There is no background except for the light. The participants do not lift themselves out of a material dimension to move towards us. They are suspended in an otherworldly dimension. They lift themselves off a background of invisibility. Even where there is ground, the participants are barely seen to touch it. What is invisible seems to us to enter the participants—to close the gap between itself and the bodies from which it has been separated. It is the supernatural essence of which Ramesar speaks (Ramesar 1997). In moving forward towards us and out through the sides of the screen it closes, for a brief moment, the gap between itself and ourselves.

Mami Wata heightens the feeling of distance, paradoxically, by maximizing the experience of proximity. The movement of the invisible in *Mami Wata* is movement from within. It works against two layers—the human body and video's body—to come to visibility. These layers are the veil or the thickness of the flesh which we encountered in *Heritage* as a porous but viscous "thisness" between the objects and ourselves. This encounter with the veil produced visibility. The gaps in the image allowed insertion. In *Mami Wata*, the objects do not invite us to encounter them as visible objects, or to co-produce their visibility. The objects control the looking by ensuring that the porosity of the veil is only available from within the frame. Invisibility enters the veil of the human body like an element unaccustomed to human form—a vast presence attempting to negotiate its way into a vessel of infinitesimal size. We do not ourselves encounter the veil, but we do witness this engagement in the movement of the body possessed. The body lends visibility to the invisible—it is the manner or mode of its appearing. In its borrowed body, the invisible presence then moves through the veil of the video until it presses against the screen.

It is after this presence has settled into the key participant's body that she begins her slow but unrelenting journey forward. Until that time there is no clear intention. Now we feel a directional and intentional consciousness expanding outwards from the subject (our object of vision) towards us and towards all other objects inside and outside of the frame. She moves thickly, trapped in viscosity. We feel that her movement is towards us but perhaps it is towards the screen—towards the limit of our consciousness. A gap is produced as the distance effected between ourselves and the object. Intentional consciousness comes from within this video and pushes out on all sides as the woman's frame exceeds the screen. As it does this, it closes the space between us. We sit transfixed. Without the dissolution of the image we see in *Heritage*, there are fewer gaps within which the consciousness of the participants can meet our own. Consciousness pushes its way forward and presses itself against us. Our encounter with the gap is an encounter from the outside. The space of the gap is filled by the other's intention.

Mami Wata gives us the scene of contemplation as a space that exists between the characters and ourselves. In *Heritage*, we enter the video to meet the characters in a space that is behind, between and within them. *Heritage* is an experience of immersion and observation. *Mami Wata* is an experience of observation and impenetrability. *Heritage* and *Mami Wata* both perform phenomenological reductions but with different results. One is probing and the other is not. One exhibits longitudinal consciousness (as characters move towards us and consciousness moves back and forth from "memory" to present) and the other latitudinal. The *horizon* of consciousness—the space in which we

Stills from *Mami Wata*. Courtesy Robert Yao Ramesar and Sonja Melton Ramesar.

meet consciousness and in which it is disclosed and becomes accessible to us—is shifted. We look on, in the opening sequence of *Mami Wata*, at drummers in extreme backlighting. The figures stand out as if against an open sky and there is no background. The absence of background produces in the viewer an effect of weightlessness—a floating dreamlike sequence which differs from the ideas of memory and dream in *Heritage* because it is not anchored in the scene of the event.

Mami Wata is ritual lifted out of its surroundings—though not out of its context—and presented to us as the present, happening now. It is the witnessing of a birth—of the previously unseen coming into visibility. The technique of removing the physical background is a process of "clearing the way" for contemplation. The video literally clears the ground and leaves only that which is intended to be the focus of our attention. The zone of contemplation exists in that space which surrounds the participants. What we confront here is a zone which surrounds the event and forces us to stay on the outside. The zone which offers contemplation itself creates a form of buffer. It allows the participants to expand further into presence without the possibility of reciprocal action on our part. We are not allowed even to mimic their actions. In a curious twist, the heightened physicality of the bodies in *Mami Wata* denies to us the type of bodily involvement in which we are engaged in *Heritage*.

In *Mami Wata*, the concretion of visibility through the bodies of the possessed suggests the existence of an essential and all-pervasive presence. It uses the human body to bring itself to visibility. Human bodies, however, are not empty vessels. Essence meets consciousness there. Essence inserts itself into the participant's body and reveals itself to the consciousness it finds there. It becomes visible to consciousness from an internal position of co-habitation. The woman turns slowly and stares, her eyes unseeing/all-seeing and wide. What we see is the woman's act of consciousness, encountering and apprehending this essence in her being. She has not yet moved towards us and her body does not fully occupy the screen. There is still distance between us. We see her through the mediation of her own body, the camera and the screen. Mediation enables vision. For the participant, there is not this distance. What the religious adherent might experience as the incorporation of a deity, we see as the incorporation of essence. In its movement, it suggests itself as an intentional force. But the movement of essence is the combined effort of its own intention and the intentional force of consciousness to which it is joined in its halting yet deliberate journey forward. Essence requires the activity and openness of individual consciousness, operationalized through the body, to come towards.

Possession, Embodiment and Consciousness

> Thus there is a paradox of immanence and transcendence in perception. Immanence, because the perceived object cannot be foreign to him who perceives; transcendence, because it always contains something more than what is actually given. And these two elements of perception are not, properly speaking, contradictory. For if we reflect on this notion of perspective, if we reproduce the perceptual experience in our thought, we see that the kind of evidence proper to the perceived, the appearance of 'something,' requires both this presence and this absence.

> – Maurice Merleau-Ponty
> (*The Visible and the Invisible*
> *[Followed by Working Notes]*, 1968: 16)

There are two forms of the real in Husserl's theory of phenomenology. The first is a type of psychological reality, which it seems is given to us in perception and in our understanding of the world in the natural attitude. The second is the reality which exists even when this first reality has been stripped away or suspended as in the transcendental reduction. Sobchack (1992) has suggested that Husserl's transcendental reduction creates an abstract and universal ego which sees and understands from a disembodied and privileged position. Such a position seems untenable to Sobchack, whose theory of cinematic identification is based on a notion of the material body as the focal point of perception and consciousness. Sobchack's interpretation of immanence or bodily reality negates the form of abstract idealism and transcendentalism which she finds in Husserl while acknowledging the possibility—and the necessity—of transcendence as a means of intersubjective communication. Yet Sobchack seems to misunderstand the productive possibilities in the notion of the transcendental as a form of present absence which underlies and underscores all that we take into evidence as existence.

Heidegger's account of the phenomenological reduction requires an understanding of the appearance of individual human beings as an appearance that is facilitated by the unseen. In Heidegger's model, the essence of individual beings is *being*. This being is the ground upon which beings become visible. The woman in *Mami Wata* is an individual being visible to us in ordinary perception. Any attempt to get at the essence of this woman must necessarily begin with our perception of her body and move towards that which makes her appearance possible. That which makes her appearance possible is invisible but always present. Heidegger's being might be seen as analogous in function to Husserl's essence. An individual being is an object as it is given to us in appearance. Husserl contends that nothing is ever given to us completely in appearance. An individual being visible to us is a particular modulation of space and time—a "certain node" in the woof of Merleau-Ponty's visible. Husserl's essence is the ground from which this particular abstract (because arbitrary) modulation springs. Essence is infinite possibility. Husserl's reduction—and Heidegger's—requires that we move beyond the object as it is given to us in ordinary perception towards its underlying essence. For Husserl, this might mean that we now perceive the object as it is intended for our vision by the essence or the invisible ground.

> Apprehension of being, ontological investigation, always turns, at first and necessarily, to some being, but then *in a precise way, it is led away* from that being *and led back to its being*. We call this basic component of phenomenological method—the leading back or reduction of investigative vision from a naively apprehended being to being—*phenomenological reduction*. (Heidegger 1988: 21)

Sobchack's immanence, in relying on what is given to us in perception, does not allow us to move through the body to an experience of its possibility. In *Mami Wata*, being intends its way through the woman's body. It also visits other participants—it shudders in the older woman and sways in the younger man. It is the backdrop of each of these individual beings—the being of their being. It manifests when there is openness-for-being. It returns to a place deep within the human body as surprisingly as it comes forth. It is as if being has come forward to show us the gap between itself and perception—between itself and the body—and has returned to the body once its mission has been completed. The task of difference has been to highlight sameness and to put into perspective the co-constitution of visibility and invisibility, of immanence and transcendence.

The transcendent is not the transcendental. Yet we might think of the transcendent as that which potentially leads us to the transcendental or opens a way towards it. I would suggest that the idea of the transcendental allows us to think about that towards which the transcendent moves and from which it ultimately proceeds—the layer of invisibility from which the visible crystallizes and comes to vision. The transcendental may exist as a layer of experience which is not uniquely accessible to a disembodied and privileged subject but is accessible to and through all bodies which are open to the possibility of the beyond. The existence of the transcendental may presuppose, not a masterful and controlling subject, but a subject cognizant of its own object-ness in the broader scheme of things. It may presuppose a subject willing to release its own intentions and to allow its being to serve as a medium for the passage of being.

It is through immanence that we arrive at the transcendental in *Mami Wata*. The transcendental is the condition of immanence. *Mami Wata* is founded on the premise of invisibility. It takes the invisible as the ground of the real. It begins with invisible presence. Heidegger's search for the being of beings—starting necessarily with "this being" or the actual body—takes us from an experience of the participant's body in the worldly attitude to an experience of the body in the otherworldly attitude. There is something in the otherworldliness of possession that gives itself over to the transcendental reduction, and the video makes full use of this by allowing us to truly see the becoming. By holding open the door to consciousness through the suspension that is the transcendental reduction, the directors release the imperative to *experience* possession and release us instead onto the imperative to see the *appearing*.[16] We are given the temporal lag as the becoming—the space for contemplation. What we see is the *act of consciousness* of possession rather than possession itself. Ramesar and Melton Ramesar convey the *journey* of consciousness into visibility.

Heidegger suggests that that which appears or does the appearing does not actually appear—does not immediately show itself—in the process of appearing. I would suggest that what is shown is its intention. In *Mami Wata*, we are held captive by presence rather than the gaze. The devotional singing facilitates this experience. We are entranced and motionless. In *Heritage*, consciousness journeys towards the present but is kept spatially within the loop of the frame. It remains in the photographic past. It is on the cusp of actualization. In *Mami Wata*, consciousness breaks out and escapes the spatial boundaries of the video. It actualizes *and* returns to virtuality of its own accord where we see the woman's face, ecstatic and peaceful, as she moves in the river. Consciousness expands into the present. Unlike consciousness in *Heritage*, which dealt with a near-past and near-present, consciousness in *Mami Wata* is not our consciousness moving back and forth, being called by the present to dislodge itself from the space of the past and so journey forward. In *Mami Wata*, it seems that consciousness belongs to being itself. This consciousness takes over the present. It expands to fill the screen and move beyond it.

This spreading out of consciousness is inhibited only by the physical limitations of the bodies themselves. The materiality of the bodies—human and video—is the curtain which consciousness encounters in its journey into the material world. We see the woman in the water, still entranced but barely moving. She seems peacefully outside of herself—calmly ecstatic. Her ankle in the water and her head above it link the body to consciousness. We have ceased to see the movement of consciousness through the woman's body coming towards us. But consciousness is still present. It now shows itself to us in the body as fragments. The return is a return to the body, but we now know that this body—deconstituted rather than decomposed—is brought together by consciousness and made material. *Mami Wata* guides our vision back from this particular being to its being—and back to the individual being again. Heidegger does not account for this final return. *Mami Wata* allows us to experience this return to the world before reflection—transformed—and so to fulfil Husserl's intention.[17] Essence inserts itself into the participant's body as an intending consciousness and reveals itself to the consciousness it finds there. It becomes visible to her individual consciousness from within. Mediation and the *epoché* give us this experience as the suspension of the woman's own consciousness and her openness to the presence of being.

Ecstasis, Temporality and the Dasein

> Time is carried away within itself as future, past, and present. As future, the Dasein is *carried away to* its past [has-been] capacity-to-be; as past [having-been], it is *carried away to* its having-been-ness; and as enpresenting, it is *carried away to* some other being or beings. Temporality as unity of future, past, and present does not carry the Dasein away just at times and occasionally; instead, as *temporality*, it is itself *the original outside-itself*, the ekstatikon. For this character of carrying-away we employ the expression the *ecstatic character* of time.
>
> – Martin Heidegger (*The Basic Problems of Phenomenology*, 1988: 267)

The Dasein provides us with a horizon of access for the disclosure of Being. It is the openness that brings Being out of concealment. The manifest or the unconcealed, when viewed in this way, comes to be understood as a form of appearing. It is not attained through a procedure of looking on the part of the viewer but through an attitude of openness on the part of the viewer to what is already present. Heidegger's framework for phenomenological seeing seems to avoid the necessity or existence of consciousness. While Husserl's reductions require the activity of consciousness directed towards itself and towards its acts of perception, Heidegger's revealing requires that we be receptive to the presence of Being. It is as if Being intends the possibility of itself being seen and merely awaits our reception of it. It seems that this intentionality—the intention of being revealed—is the very condition of Being.

Mami Wata allows us to integrate and extend Heidegger's being and Being into Husserl's ideas surrounding the perception of the object. In *Mami Wata*, the individual consciousness of the woman surrenders itself as she adopts the attitude of the Dasein. As the Dasein becomes the woman's *mode* of consciousness, the consciousness that belongs to being intends its way through her body. The consciousness that belongs to being allows us to perceive the body of this woman as a modulation of space and time made possible by the invisible being now intending its way through it. The woman's body—the *object as it is intended*—in turn brings being to visibility. The consciousness that we see intending its way through the participant's body is not visible as much as it *comes to visibility*. It is unconcealed—its presence is made known—without being fully visible. It is visible only on and through the body of the participant. Yet the body acts as a screen that blocks its full and unhindered passage. In this way, to follow Heidegger, being is simultaneously concealed and unconcealed. The being of the participant is revealed and concealed through the body.

What is revealed in *Mami Wata* is experienced both as the being of the participant and the operative consciousness of Being that is its generative ground. Young (2002) suggests that it was Heidegger's intention that Being and being be "thought together" as complementary but not identical. Young opts to convey this relation by using the formulation B/being. But being, supposedly, does not itself "presence." *Mami Wata* suggests otherwise. The presencing of being through the body of the participant—and the facilitation of this process through the openness of consciousness—is a reminder that Ramesar's videos extend our understanding of the possibility of phenomenological experience. Video's mediation allows reflection—and interpretation of the event unfolding. We do not directly experience the Dasein—what we see is the *participant's* openness—and the path that this clears for the presencing of her being. Her openness-for-Being seems to facilitate the operation which brings being forward and through the body. Suspended animation and the absence of background allow this process to appear for us as an unfolding through time.

Time is the horizon for the understanding of Being. Time is also the basic constitution of the Dasein. As such, time both opens us up to the manifestation of Being and determines how we will understand it. Yet time is not to be understood as a series of discrete, measurable units. The time which underlies the experience and possibility of Being and the Dasein is indivisible. It is cyclical and constantly in motion. It is outside itself as it is carried away simultaneously towards past, present and future. This time—Temporality—is forever becoming. This Temporality, forever carried away, is Heidegger's *ekstatikon*. The horizon of the ecstasis in *Mami Wata*—that towards which time is carried away and disclosed—is a horizon of the present. *Mami Wata* allows us to dwell in the transcendental reduction and in the experience of ecstasy—to witness the process of becoming as a profoundly present experience. We do not see consciousness. We do not see B/being. We see B/being's intention as an act of becoming.

Stills from *Mami Wata*. Courtesy Robert Yao Ramesar and Sonja Melton Ramesar.

The woman entranced in *Mami Wata* is outside of time. She is ecstatic. She is transported to this experience by the very possibility of the Dasein or openness-for-Being. Heidegger suggests that the horizonal-ecstatic character of time makes intentionality possible. The horizon of each ecstasis (past, present and future) is the *open expanse towards which* remotion (this act of carrying-away) is outside itself (Heidegger 1988: 267). Remotion opens up the horizon and keeps it open. There is a double ecstatic moment taking place in *Mami Wata*. The act of possession takes the participant outside of herself. The lengthening effected by slow motion also takes time outside of itself. This combination produces a situation in which ecstasy is experienced by the viewer as B/being moving towards us in the present. We are confronted with the horizon of the ecstasis as a kind of boundary condition that straddles the border between visibility and invisibility.[18] The horizon of the ecstasis serves a function similar to that of the veil in *Heritage*. In *Mami Wata*, the horizon stretches itself before the onset of B/being's intentional consciousness. The horizonal-ecstatic character of time allows B/being to intend its way towards us in the present.

In *Mami Wata*, we watch time unfold. We witness from a distance. In *Heritage*, we are *in* time. We join the procession. When we are *in* time we do not experience ecstasis. It is necessary first to open oneself to the Temporality of the Dasein—to the possibility of standing outside of time—and to the possibility of Being. The directors give us *time* in which to witness the becoming. This time accentuates the lag between the perception of the object and the reflection on the act of perception—an extended stay within the psychological reduction and the distance necessary for contemplation. Two different cameras were used to shoot the scenes in *Mami Wata*. The effect is another layer of distance which contributes to an experience of dream and suspension. In *Heritage*, the world is suspended and this literally allows us to move differently through time. In *Mami Wata*, there is further bracketing of the world, but we do not move. We are able to stand as witnesses in contemplation on our own acts of consciousness. If we hold what we perceive and the act in which it is perceived, we allow the temporal lag to join the space of contemplation between the participants and ourselves and so contribute to the expansive space of consciousness. We are witness to a broadening into the world. We suspend our concern with the world in order to integrate consciousness more fully into that world.

Heritage allows the intention of the characters to meet our own. In *Mami Wata*, the consciousness of the participants appears to be suspended or put aside. The participants themselves appear to have bracketed their experience of the world—the mundane. The consciousness that is there does not meet us at all. We are caught up in the details of a dress, a head-tie, a scarf and are returned to reflection upon the act of consciousness and the unfolding of time, on how it is that we see these details so clearly. We are caught up in the perception of light and shadow. We see the pouring of the oil onto the offerings and the flowers that lie beneath. We see all this in slow motion and the main character moves towards us. The slow motion shows her coming forward and moving back. This is B/being coming into the material realm. Time is lengthened further and the gap is held. We do not—cannot—enter the space between the slip of the dress and the slide of the feet, the turn of the head and the brush of the hand. This distance is given to us—not co-constituted with our participation. The stereoscopic-type views of *Heritage* offer a series of sliding, gliding characters moving along the surface of the image and several layers deep. Yet in *Heritage*, the figures come from within the image towards us and the illusion of layers comes from that act of proceeding from within. In *Mami Wata*, the stereoscopic perspective is heightened. The figures do not exist inside of the image—they float along its surface and carry our perceptions and acts of consciousness with them.

When the main participant is in the water, we meet her there but we have not seen her enter. It is a rare moment in which the video does not cut to produce continuity but to shift location. This shift in consciousness and physical location suggests a sense of completion. We see an ankle, her shoulders, her face—eyes closed—still ecstatic. The journey continues in ways which we cannot access. I can no longer see the movement of consciousness through space, moving towards me as towards a future. Instead, I see the internal workings of consciousness reflected in the face of a woman. She turns her head from side to side. She exists—subsists—within the river and images are reflected there. Her suspension of the mundane has been internalized in the body. Consciousness has returned to her space of reflection and experience, inaccessible to my methods. My own *epoché* is enhanced by this limitation. It is forced to confront the mutuality that is needed for vision—the mutuality of intention. Without it there is nothing visible. In *Mami Wata*, the veil is pushed out towards us by intending consciousness. The gap is wider though the opening is smaller. The movement towards us diminishes the point of access for *our* entry but broadens the horizon of access for the exit of consciousness.

Stills from *Journey To Ganga Mai*. Courtesy the artist.

CHAPTER 3
BEING, CONSCIOUSNESS AND TIME

How does time make itself felt in a shot? It becomes tangible when you sense something significant, truthful, going on beyond the events on the screen; when you realize, quite consciously, that what you see in the frame is not limited to the visual depiction, but is a pointer to something stretching out beyond the frame and to infinity; a pointer to life.

– Andrei Tarkovsky (*Sculpting in Time*, 1986: 117–118)

Journey to Ganga Mai opens with a mid-level, multi-coloured shot of fabric— green and red and yellow clothing. The image is slightly blurred. There are several people standing close together in a small crowd. We do not see their faces. It is outdoors and the sun is shining. The music is devotional singing. There is a trembling, rippling effect on the clothes that magnifies the sense of closeness. The camera pulls out haltingly and the bodies are visible in full height but obscured by the appearance of text in the foreground. We see that the bodies are ankle deep in water. The rippling effect on the clothes is echoed in the rippling of the water. The text explains that Ganga Dashara celebrates the coming of the Goddess of the river[19] to earth from the Himalayas—and that among the rituals performed is the shaving of babies' first hair. In the background, there is a ghost trail—it is a burst of colour emanating from the core (of the participants) and spreading like the visible trace of a staccato movement. In the background, also, there is chanting.

Following this there is white-out. In the next scene, the camera hovers over a brown river. A coconut husk bearing offerings is being released into the water by a pair of hands. The wrists and lower arms are covered with bracelets and the ends of a sari drape over them. They are reds and oranges and earthy hues and gold. The camera shot encompasses the husk drifting off to the right and the releasing hands off to the left. The title of the video appears in the middle. Another pair of hands is seen at the left and the camera moves slowly up to reveal the two women who have released the offering. The camera follows their movement as they stand from their bent position over the offering. They clasp their hands as they gesture in namaste. *We see them in profile. We see them follow the movement of the husk with their eyes. We sense one continuous motion from left to right across the river. The river seems to carry the action along. Another white-out changes the image.*

This time, the camera focuses on a lone woman, bent, perhaps in prayer. She appears to stoop or kneel in front of an offering. She is not in the water but on the shore. She is wearing a yellow blouse. Her head is covered and we see her from behind. The camera pulls out, again haltingly. We then see the woman in close-up and profile. Her hands are clasped in prayer. What follows is a series of images that seems to flow effortlessly—with no particular narrative order but a certain intrinsic connectedness. The video is in slow motion and shot in daylight, but there is no stark contrast. Trees, the sky and the river form the background. Several of the shots are but a few seconds long, yet they seem to be filled with time. It is as if a common rhythm—the rhythm of the river—permeates every scene and fills every action with duration. The chanting continues in a loop. Lighted deyas[20] *are set on the water and the shore. A man performs* aarti[21]. *The circular motion of the round brass plate is at one with the rhythm of image and sound.*

Several participants perform aarti. *Others walk to specific sites of worship or release offerings into the river. At times, the camera follows their movements. A woman pours water into the river from a* lota[22]. *We see the pouring water close up and in slow motion as it cascades down and makes contact with the river. It is as if the water—and everything in the scene—is returning to its source. A man in animal skin is dancing. He carries a trident and seems to exist outside of the main action. This breaks the rhythm somewhat because his movements are not slow and deliberate like those of the others. But he seems to be an integral part of the scene. A woman releases another husk. The chanting continues. Chanting and action are looped. We see hands in* namaste, *hands releasing offerings. A bright yellow cloth appears on the screen. It is held—suspended—over the* water by women. The cloth is full, but we cannot see its contents. It stretches longitudinally into the frame and towards us.

The participants seldom face us directly, but a toddler breaks this trend. He is held—we assume by his father—as he has his hair cut. Several women surround him. We come upon the action from behind. We see the blade as it neatly shaves his almost-bald head. The contact of blade on skin is almost mesmerizing. His father kisses him. His mother plays with a lock of his hair. As the shaving continues, the camera cuts to a bundle of his locks caught in a red and orange sari by a woman standing just behind. The move to the sari is almost seamless. His haircut complete, he turns to look at us. He is holding a camera. We see him and the camera close up. He smiles and moves to take a picture. We are framed. We are suddenly made aware that we are not part of the scene. Until now we have moved unconsciously with the flow of the action. There has been no gap to indicate our distance/difference. The boy's perception of us makes us aware of ourselves as objects of vision.

The offerings continue but in no particular order. There is no discernible past or future, and most actions appear to have merged into one. We return to the stream—of consciousness, action and the river. They appear to be one and the same. The action is repetitive—as is the sound. At times we see the same participants, at other times not. The action seems almost non-intentional because it appears to be directed nowhere. It is directed towards regeneration—towards itself. Movement here does not cover distance—it covers time. We see over a woman's shoulder as the camera captures in close-up another vessel pouring water into the river. She is pouring, but we make that connection obliquely. We see fragments, close up, and are made to intuit the whole. At the mouth of the lota is a single lilac flower. It tumbles out ahead of the water and we seem to see it fall in real time, a time in which we experience the flower's movement as our own. A pundit places a tikkaa[23] on the forehead of a celebrant. His movement is followed by the camera. It is all a flow of images and sound. Participants sit and sing in a covered space near the banks of the river. They are surrounded by deyas. The yellow cloth returns, and this time we see that it is filled with flowers. The women sift through them, rearranging them in scooping and lifting motions.

A woman with a tambourine dances. We focus on her full body and then on her feet. Like the male dancer before her, she appears to be somewhat at odds with the general flow of the action but seems to be an integral part of the event. It is a moment that serves to interrupt our own flow of consciousness, but the flow continues. There *are long shots of the river. Close-ups show a single flower, a coconut husk, the flame of a deya. They each float along the river, suspended. The camera follows. Much happens on the surface of this river. We are of the scene but not immersed. We see but do not contemplate. The flow is continuous and carries us along, away. We recognize participants from earlier scenes, but do we experience memory? Time exists as past, present and future here. A foot exits the water and we see it at ankle level. On land, people are leaving, also in streams, and the event begins to dissolve. The flow is broken by a banner that sends a message to "Mother Earth." The image of the man with the trident returns and in between the credits we return to the scene of the* tikkaa *being placed on the forehead. It is still a slow, steady stream of images. An offering is released and, starting with their hands, we recognize the offerers as the women of the title scene. We see them in full now. Our journey has taken us back to the beginning.*

Journey to Ganga Mai is not a phenomenological reduction but the presentation of the generative ground from which all reductions are made and to which they return. This ground is the river—the source and the condition of possibility. It is Being, allowed to surface as the phenomenologically reduced. *Journey to Ganga Mai* does not present to us the reflective conversion, the *epoché* or the eidetic reduction. It *brackets* these processes so that we might dwell in their culmination. It does not present a space for reflection on consciousness. Instead, *Journey to Ganga Mai* presents a ritual event as a never-ending unfolding that moves towards itself as the fulfilment of intention. *Journey to Ganga Mai* is the ultimate reduction—the leading back to oneself.

The Enfoldment in Time

Heidegger describes the Dasein as futural—it understands itself in terms of its capacity to be. The essence of the future lies in coming-towards-oneself. The Dasein, therefore, must take cognizance of the present and the past as the conditions upon which the future might exist. It must understand itself in relation to the past, which it is no longer, and the present in which it must dwell. *Journey to Ganga Mai* provides an opportunity for witnessing the result of the Dasein's movement towards itself. Through its circular narrative and repetitive soundtrack, the video folds in upon itself. The participants do not come towards us or break out of the frame. Two devotees in the title frame follow with their eyes the movement of the offering to the right of the frame along the river and, we imagine, out of our view. All that is sent upon the river will eventually return—in the present form or another. It is the camera's constant return to the river that seems to guarantee this. What floats out of the frame is not lost. The journey begins again. The action in *Journey* is directed inward and is supported by the participants' meditative actions of devotion and the experience of time within the video.

Sound can influence the perception of time through temporal animation, temporal linearization or vectorization (Chion 2000). Animation suggests movement. Linearization suggests causation—a beginning, middle and end of action. Vectorization establishes a feeling of movement towards a future. Vectorization is our primary experience in *Journey to Ganga Mai*. In this video, the repetitive phrasing on the soundtrack echoes.[24] The movement towards the future is made all the more insistent by the fact that the sound is not instrumental but sung. We recognize the phrases. Each incantation of "Om Namah Sivaya" precedes what we know by now will follow. The singing moves forward only to return to itself. In *Journey to Ganga Mai*, the chanting is the only sound and the echo serves to establish a sort of cocoon, suggesting that the scene is shut off from the world and is in fact its own world enfolding upon itself. The singing surrounds the action and our experience of it.

The influence of sound is facilitated by structural elements in the video. As we saw in *Heritage*, the microrhythms of the disintegrating, depixellated image created a "trembling temporality." In *Journey*, the microrhythm of the river is ever-present and is reinforced by the recurrence and circularity of several ritual gestures, principally the movement of the brass plate during the performance of *aarti*. The effect of this movement is to create a subtle distance between the plate and the river. At the same time, it complements the movement of the river. The same is true of the pouring of libations into the water. The movement cuts directly into the movement of the river (vertical into horizontal) and would seem to be at cross purposes with the river. But it is complementary. Both the plate and the *lota* stand apart from the background (the river) at the moment when the act of movement is performed, yet they seem also to be returning to their source. It is as if these movements were secondary phrases in the overarching sound and movement template that is the singing and the river. The separation from the background is temporary and serves to highlight their similarity and difference. The subtle distance is a subtle gap which brings to our

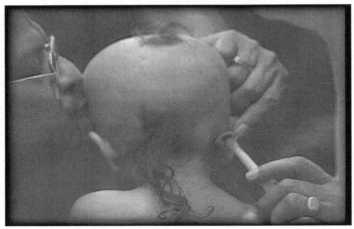

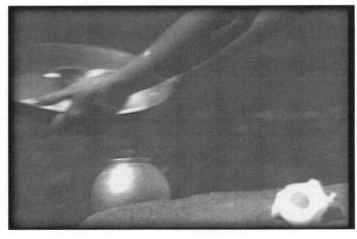

Stills from *Journey To Ganga Mai*. Courtesy the artist.

attention the condition for the possibility of vision. Through Ramesar's cutting on motion, one action seems to blend into another from one image to the next. This contributes to the fluidity of motion and creates a sense of movement into the future but also an experience of timelessness—of time moving into itself. In this video, sound and image combine to produce a heightened sense of Temporality.

The pundit's singing is incantatory. This incantation produces a state similar to dream. An associative rhythm in the editing is facilitated by the river, the movements of the participants and the cuts on motion (Dermody 1995). The images in *Journey to Ganga Mai* are not the stereoscopic views of *Mami Wata* or *Heritage*. The participants here are not lifted out of the stream of the river that is the backdrop of this piece. Instead, they are *in* the stream and appear to be drawn out of it only to appear on its surface, even when on the ground, as if attached by some invisible filament. We are awakened by the toddler and his camera taking pictures of us. The boy's camera inserts distance. We suddenly become objects of vision. We are awakened also by the dancers. In a move that is atypical of our experience of the video, we find ourselves looking on at these figures, contemplating them and reflecting on the act of seeing. The camera approaches at a low angle, exploring in a way that is unfamiliar to us here. Although we view them also in slow motion, the dancers appear to experience a time that is not quite of the video. They twirl and stamp but do not flow in a rhythm synchronous with the general rhythmic pattern of the piece. The dancers seem to remind us of the existence of a world of time outside of the frame. In so doing, they remind us that we exist as viewers within the already reduced space and time of the video. We dwell with the images and within the video. *Journey to Ganga Mai* takes us straight to the heart of the transcendental reduction without our being aware.

Journey does not fit neatly into the stages of the phenomenological reduction. *Heritage* facilitated the reflective conversion and highlighted the temporal lag wherein our consciousness met the consciousness of the characters and our bodies joined the scene. The gap was the point of access. In *Mami Wata*, the video performed a transcendental reduction or *epoché* which lengthened and strengthened the conversion, allowing for deep contemplation on the way in which the invisible as B/being and essence came into visibility. *Mami Wata* formed a bridge across the transcendental and eidetic reductions. The gap allowed the exit of consciousness rather than our entry into the scene. *Journey to Ganga Mai* is a reduction which does not lead to contemplation on mental acts or acts of consciousness. Instead, it allows us to experience immersion in the stream of consciousness. *Journey to Ganga Mai* is suspension as a peculiar form of bracketing in which the world is drawn *into* the video rather than merely being relegated to a position outside of it. The video exhibits the characteristics of the Dasein and of Heidegger's manifestation as an appearing accomplished not through mental acts but through an attitude of openness. We have entered the scene although we have no cognitive or bodily memory of having done so. The video exists for us as that space of openness that is the Dasein.

In *Mami Wata*, we experience one woman's openness-for-*Being* as an openness-to-*being*—the being of an individual human being intends its way towards us together with consciousness. In *Journey to Ganga Mai*, we experience the Dasein—conceived of as our *own* openness-for-*Being*. We do not witness the being of individuals coming into visibility. Instead, individual beings are seen to dwell in the underlying presence—the river—that makes their appearance possible. The video suggests the existence of this presence at the heart of the participants. It reveals this presence in the opening shot when a ghost trail of rainbow colours is drawn from them. This image is captured in still as the explanatory text is laid over it. It is the background upon which we literally read the text. There is no exaggerated contrast in *Journey to Ganga Mai*—no sharp delineation between subjects and their field. As a result, the gaps which appeared in *Heritage* and *Mami Wata* as spaces surrounding the characters/participants, lifting them out of their background, are not present here. The celebrants subsist in the stream of movement and are surrounded by a type of generative ground that is experienced as the river. *Being* is the manifest grasped in conjunction with the hidden side of reality (Young 2002: 17). We see the celebrants (the manifest) in conjunction with the hidden side of reality. They subsist one in the other. We find ourselves subsisting in the stream without a sense of the process which has brought us here. While the experience of subsisting suggests a transcendental reduction in which we dwell, the video has not given to us the strategies which led to this dwelling. We have brought ourselves, through the Dasein, to Heidegger's manifestation of Being.

In Heidegger's formulation, the actualization of time as a simultaneously occurring past, present and future keeps the horizon (of disclosure) open and reinforces our openness-for-Being. Heidegger's three ecstases of past, present and future belong together "intrinsically and with co-equal originality" (Heidegger

1988: 267). *Journey to Ganga Mai* helps us to see this belonging. The mantra closes off distractions and opens us up to the possibility of recurring, indivisible time. It offers us distance from the world and a retreat from regular temporality. *Journey* heightens the experience of Temporality and so facilitates access to the experience of Being. Time accretes in *Journey* and stretches out alongside itself. Human bodies are *in* time and exist in the video as part of the unending flow of time. The Dasein, or the openness-for-Being, *is* time. In Heidegger's terms, it is the "how" and not the "what" of being temporal. Ramesar gives us *time* in *Journey to Ganga Mai* and the entire video replicates the experience of the Dasein.

Being is found in the background. It exists *as* visibility—it does not come to visibility—through the river. Its constituents—the celebrants—come forth from this background only to return. They are Merleau-Ponty's nodes in the woof of the simultaneous and the successive, coming forward to show their proper existence as part of the invisible. Their concretion in visibility is only temporary but their im/permanence endures. And though we watch from the outside, we feel ourselves to be part of the enduring. We float, like the participants, along the river. We are carried along in the Dasein. We follow the movement of the pouring libation and the razor against the toddler's shaved head. He is initially turned away from us while we see his parents in profile flanking him on either side. We sit mesmerized rather than completely immobilized. We are suspended in time like the yellow fabric held aloft by the female devotees. It is a stream that comes towards us—or moves into the video. We see almost no beginning and no end—the camera provides just enough focus to allow the fabric to occupy the screen. Certain objects—the toddler's head, the lilac flower, the fabric—call out subtly to us. They exist in the stream in peculiar ways—all at right angles to the flow of the river. They cross the stream of Being's consciousness only to draw us in. The flower falls. The razor comes down. The boy turns his head towards us. The suspension effected in *Journey* allows not merely contemplation but the possibility of fusion.

In *Journey to Ganga Mai*, there is no veil that we perceive in halting movements of the camera. There is no viscosity through which we struggle to attain vision. Instead, the trembling temporality of the river suggests itself as the possibility for vision that it offers up freely. The river stands in for our experience of the veil—as the medium that makes vision possible—but seems to offer no resistance. In *Journey to Ganga Mai*, there seems to be no room for our consciousness but intentionality exists still. It is felt in the repetitive phrasing of

Stills from *Journey To Ganga Mai*. Courtesy the artist.

the *kirtan*—the devotional chanting—and in the relentless movement forward and into itself that is the video. Consciousness is very much present in *Journey to Ganga Mai*, but it reveals itself as a journey inward. The elements lifted out of the stream of river and consciousness glide along these surfaces. And in the midst of this movement, there is stillness. *Journey* creates the illusion of time that simultaneously moves and stands still. Bergson suggests that "to perceive is to immobilize" (Bergson 1988: 208). *Journey* lifts the sedimentation of our habitual viewing and allows us to truly see.

Bergson (1965) suggests that two perceptions are simultaneous if they can be apprehended in the same mental act. In *Journey to Ganga Mai*, our experience of the flow of the event and our experience of the elements in it are apprehended in a single mental act. There is no separation in experience except at the times when we are confronted by the boy-photographer and the dancers. At these times, we are aware of two flows of time that exist as discrete entities for our consciousness. They are contemporaneous—not simultaneous—and do not exist within our duration. Real time is experienced and perceived. It is experienced as succession and continuity rather than a series of instants. Real time is duration—a continuity of consciousness. In *Journey to Ganga Mai*, we feel our consciousness enduring. Circularity and repetition allow us to believe that it is *time* rather than the event that is unfolding. We might think of the fulfilment of time—its actualization as past, present and future—as the fulfilment of Being's intention. This time has no end.

Being, Consciousness and Time

> Look at slavery and so on and the role of dreaming and transcendence...look at the transcendence in possession in Orisha, in Hinduism (in Kali Puja)...there's always that state of dreaming and the spirit...that will always transcend the material realities of what we're going through.... It's just found a new form, but the spirit continues. And that was my thing—to *rendez-vous* with that particular space and time—timelessness.
>
> – Robert Yao Ramesar (Interview with the author, 2004)

71

Journey to Ganga Mai invites a mystical experience. It is a window onto the transcendental. It is an experience of union, not with the characters, but with Being and with time itself. Of the three videos discussed in this book, *Journey to Ganga Mai* expresses most clearly Ramesar's intention to "*rendez-vous* with timelessness." Roger McLure (2005) suggests that, while phenomenologists may differ in their attachment to particular notions of time and its passing, they are all concerned with the concept of a fundamental or original time—a time before times—and that they seek to render time visible or present. *Journey to Ganga Mai* makes fundamental time visible as an encounter with timelessness. In so doing, it brings us closer to an experience of the transcendental. Our ordinary experience of time is an experience of a serial unfolding. As Heidegger suggests, human *beings* are *in* time and encounter time as discrete and measurable units. The Dasein—openness-for-*Being*—*is* time. It is not in it. But *Being* is also "the open." It is transcendental. It is more than—and the condition of possibility of—our apprehension of individual beings (Young 2002). It is not easily grasped by systematic reductions but intuited in an experience of contact and immediacy—characteristics of mystical experience.

Daniel So writes of mystical experience as an experience taking place in "a peculiar mode of consciousness" (So 2001: 1), making a claim for the epistemic value of mysticism—for mysticism as an order of knowledge. *Journey to Ganga Mai*—through its own material body and presentation—affords us an opportunity to theorize these connections. The work of the reduction is not evident in this video—we come to the encounter through a door that has been held wide open. We do not work our way through the gap. The video *is* the gap. It is consciousness held open through a series of time-lengthening gestures of *aarti*, libation and offering in slow motion. In the mystical mode of consciousness, there is knowledge of a totality that is not easily reduced. In *Journey to Ganga Mai*, we recognize the river as an unending source. We see the participants in the stream and emerging out of it. We feel ourselves immersed and at the same time carried along. We are immersed, not in the video, but in the stream as Being that draws us *in* towards itself and *along* beyond the visible boundaries of the video's frame. Where the intending consciousness of being pushed out towards us in *Mami Wata*, the consciousness of Being in *Journey to Ganga Mai* pulls us in. In *Mami Wata*, the consciousness of being intended its way through the woman's body and revealed itself to us as the being of *this* being. The consciousness of Being in *Journey to Ganga Mai* intends its way along the river and reveals itself to us as the underlying possibility of being and beings. It is the source from which they—and we—emerge. We do not experience each devotee as a purely discrete entity but as part of a general, indivisible flow of consciousness made material. Being both constitutes and exceeds us.

Journey to Ganga Mai is an irreducible givenness (Carlson 2007: 155) that exceeds the frame. This video is *given to us*—it is not called into consciousness by our own intention. It exists as a call. The response to the call—to enter into and dwell in the experience of fundamental time—is subsumed within the very existence of that call.[25] It is here that our consciousness meets a consciousness that exceeds. *Journey to Ganga Mai* is a "concretion of visibility" of consciousness itself. Ramesar's videos perform a phenomenological investigation in which consciousness is incrementally revealed. In *Heritage*, the video performs a psychological reduction or reflective conversion, bracketing the mundane. The temporal lag persists as a reminder of the distance between our reflection on the act of consciousness and the perceptual act itself—and our consciousness enters there. In *Mami Wata*, we experience the process of coming to visibility as the work of embodiment and consciousness. *Mami Wata* lengthens the reduction and provides a space for the exit of being's consciousness as a consciousness that exists beyond our own. In *Journey to Ganga Mai*, consciousness of separation is suspended. We are conjoined and immersed. The act of consciousness is given to us *as* the perceptual act itself. It is "direct and reflective perceptual experience" (Sobchack 1992: 9) made material and presented to us *as* the video.

Consciousness in Husserl is always intentional—it is always consciousness *of* something. And in the reduction we reflect on the acts of consciousness that bring the object of investigation towards us. Heidegger suggests that we come to the phenomenologically revealed through openness and reception. But where Heidegger moves beyond consciousness in favour of the existence of Being, Ramesar's video inserts consciousness as/at the heart of Being. It presents the consciousness of Being as a consciousness directed towards itself and towards the future. In *Journey to Ganga Mai*, this consciousness *intends* that we *receive* it. The consciousness that belongs to Being intends us also—and draws us in. Being's consciousness is consciousness of—and intention towards—all being and all beings and of no being whatsoever. It is the fulfilment of Husserl's eidetic reduction—recognition of the infinite possibilities of the real. An object is never fully given to us in perception, but we intend its wholeness through acts of intuition. Being's intention is a reaching towards and an intuition of wholeness. Being is made present but does not itself "presence." Being's intention in *Journey to Ganga Mai* is a mode of appearing. It is the "how" and not the "what" of that appearing.

Heidegger conceives of the metaphysical in terms of a transcendental that is source—exceeding both being and beings yet tied irrevocably to them (Young 2002). Immanence and transcendence are intertwined. The transcendental is the concealed and the unconcealed. *Journey to Ganga Mai* offers contact with this experience of un/concealment as a form of knowledge. It is knowledge that goes beyond reflection on the acts of consciousness which bear the object towards us. It is knowledge beyond our intention. It is *not* knowledge *of*. It is knowledge *as* existence. Vision here exists as a conduit for apprehension—closing the gap between perception and the act which brings it to us. It is Husserl's "pure seeing" taken up as an experience of revelation.

Journey to Ganga Mai makes explicit the notion of the mystical that haunts so many phenomenological writings. Husserl explores the possibility of contact with "the things themselves"—through the reduction—in their intuitive givenness. Heidegger seeks the possibility of contact with Being—through dwelling—as it manifests. Each strategy assumes the existence of a presence that is more than is given to us in appearance. In *Journey to Ganga Mai*, a woman pours water out of a *lota* into the river. A lilac flower falls. In the slow and cyclical motion of the video, we experience this duration as our own—in a time before times made visible. We see the woman in fragments only and intuit that it is she who pours. Woman, flower and water are part of the unending and underlying stream of river and consciousness of which we are a part. As constitutive background of all that appears, this stream is Being. It is Being, consciousness and fundamental time revealed as conditions for the possibility of mystical experience.

CONCLUSION

Every intellectual experience, indeed every experience whatsoever, can be made into an object of pure seeing an apprehension while it is occurring. *And in this act of seeing it is an absolute givenness.* It is given as an existing entity, as a "this-here." It would make no sense at all to doubt its being.

– Edmund Husserl (*The Idea of Phenomenology*, 1999: 24)

Phenomenology offers to us a way of *encountering* the video object. It also offers to video a way of exploring the world that it presents to us for vision. Phenomenology aims to move beyond the mere appearance of things towards an apprehension of how they come to be in the world for us. Edmund Husserl, Martin Heidegger and Maurice Merleau-Ponty each offer a unique approach to phenomenological investigation. For Husserl, the key to phenomenological investigation is the phenomenological reduction which focuses attention on the act of consciousness that brings the object into the world for us. It brackets or suspends our belief in the relevance of the external world and probes the object for what it might reveal to us about its essence. The reduction leads us to a reflection on our subjective experience of the object and on the way in which that experience co-constitutes the object *as* an object for our perception. For Heidegger, the phenomenological reduction is the leading back from a naïve apprehension of individual beings towards a more profound apprehension of the being of those beings. The method of the reduction and its link to consciousness are de-emphasized in favour of an attitude of openness-for-Being in which Being—as ultimate ground—is allowed to manifest itself to us. In Merleau-Ponty's phenomenology, our gaze is directed towards the object as a material body in the world, endowed with consciousness. The object reaches out to the world—and to our consciousness in the world—and is implicated in it. The object is not reduced but comes to our perception through a mutual act of vision. Merleau-Ponty probes the consciousness of the object as it intends its way towards us and offers itself to us for vision.

The videos of Robert Yao Ramesar demonstrate the intertwining of these three approaches and extend the scope of phenomenological investigation. How does video make visible the act of looking and the act of being seen? How does it intimate the presence of that which cannot be seen? What is the role of video's material body in facilitating this process? Ramesar's videos open us onto the possibility of a "pure seeing" through reflection and meditation—both on vision and on the acts of consciousness that make that vision possible. They offer to us contact with vision as a process of becoming. They *enact* phenomenology as method in the process of intending their way into the world, restoring us to that world by bringing the trace of presence, consciousness and perception through their material bodies. Ramesar's uniqueness as a film-maker generally—and as a Caribbean film-maker specifically—is to have imbued the video object with a subjective consciousness all its own. Video, in this work, brings forth an experience of consciousness that forces contemplation on the kind of object that video might be in the world.

Video's ontology—the nature of its being in the world—is at once immanent and transcendent. It is embodied consciousness unfolding through time and enfolding us in time to bring forward the trace of Being. It is the indexical trace of presence. The videos' camera takes hold of and transmits to us the visible along with the invisible—it makes *known* the idea of presence through visibility itself. These videos therefore pose an epistemological question as well: How do we come to knowledge—and what is it possible to know—through the moving image? It is video's body that brings to us the expression of intention and consciousness as the expression of its own perception of the world. It makes phenomenology's methods visible and material to us. Video's intending consciousness probes and contemplates the object, making seeing visible. Phenomenological method is not only carried out *through* the body of the video, it is presented to us *as* the body of video. Video *mediates*—and its materiality makes possible the presencing of B/being. Video is phenomenology's material presence in the world before us, made manifest and concrete.

I understand Caribbeing as an attempt to restore—and re-situate—a particular way of seeing as a way of being-in-the-world. Ramesar's videos clear a path through the natural attitude of forgetting—our failure in "colonial, rationalist convention" to *re-cognize* the material in conjunction with the non-material. They invite us to *perceive*—and to reflect on the acts of consciousness that bring that perception to us. They move us towards a philosophical attitude in which knowledge itself—and knowledge *as* self—is presented. Objects address us *as* a world—a world that co-constitutes them for vision. They call out to us and offer themselves to us for vision. They resist our gaze. They invite us in. Their consciousness comes forward to meet our own. The encounter with these videos is an encounter with vision and experience—materiality, perception and consciousness. These videos extend our work in both cinema and philosophy by suggesting a theory of encounter grounded in embodied consciousness and a metaphysics of presence.

Stills from *Heritage: A Wedding In Moriah*. Courtesy the artist.

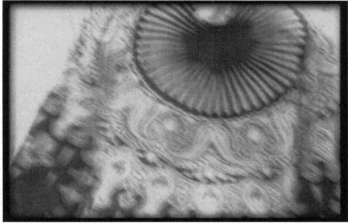

Stills from *Mami Wata*. Courtesy Robert Yao Ramesar and Sonja Melton Ramesar.

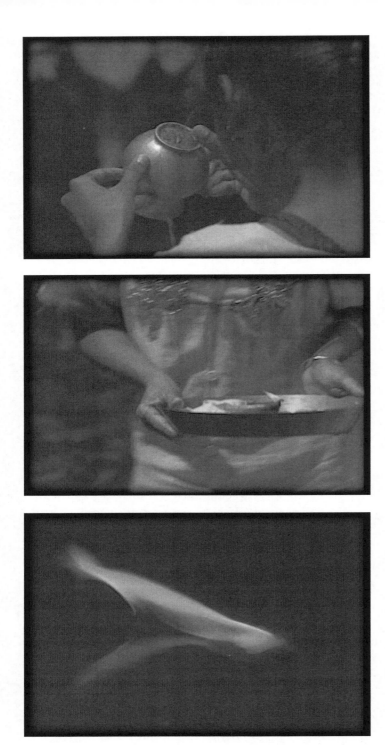

Stills from *Journey To Ganga Mai*. Courtesy the artist.

ENDNOTES

1. Solarization over-exposes film to light in the early stages of processing. It produces an effect of indistinct, aqueous, voluminous patches, shimmering with a kind of inner resonance. It is precisely the kind of effect that one could utilize to convey an experience of essence or inner core. Objects seem somehow turned inside out—what is essential or beyond further reduction is made visible or put on display. Ramesar produces this effect on video in post-production.

2. Ramesar is recognized professionally as a film-maker. Like many film-makers, he produces work on video. He blurs the boundaries, applying film techniques— such as solarization—to video. I will use the term film-maker throughout this book. The term video accurately describes the format of the work discussed, and video's malleability and materiality are important to the aesthetic innovations outlined here.

3. The few book-length studies which include—or focus on—cinema in the Anglophone Caribbean (e.g. Warner 2000 and Cham 1992) tend to address questions of identity, representation and historical or production context.

4. While I acknowledge the important work that is being done on the role of the non-visual senses in our experience of cinema, it is primarily vision which concerns me here. My focus is on the convergence of Husserl's "pure seeing"— together with Heidegger's "showing" and Merleau-Ponty's "look"—and the revelatory seeing which Ramesar attempts to initiate through his Caribbeing aesthetic.

5. Ihde (1976) provides an excellent overview from which I have sourced this interpretation. Ihde also suggests that the phenomenological concerns and methods of Husserl and Heidegger are dialectically related and overlap, Heidegger's method picking up where Husserl's leaves off. Ramesar's videos allow us to see this connection.

6. Although Dasein is often translated as "being there," Lovitt (1977: xxxv n2) cites a letter from Heidegger to Prof. J. Glenn Gray, written in 1972, in which he expresses his preference for the term "openness" as a translation of the "da" in Dasein. Heidegger is said to have indicated that there is a turning from "consciousness" towards "openness-for-Being" without which his work is misunderstood. Heidegger (2001: 3–4 and 144) also elaborates on this issue in letters to Medard Boss. Here he does not negate the significance of the translation "there" but explains that the Dasein is both temporality and spatiality. He talks of a "holding open" which is more than a physical location in space. It is a capacity to receive and perceive the significance of things given to it. This is the sense in which I choose to interpret Dasein here.

7. *Heritage: A Wedding in Moriah* and *Journey to Ganga Mai* were produced as part of the television documentary series *People*, through the government's Information Division. *Mami Wata* was produced independently in 1992 and re-edited in 1996. It was directed by Robert Yao Ramesar and Sonja Melton. (Melton is now known professionally as Sonja Melton Ramesar and that is the name that will be used in discussing her contribution here.) All videos were shot in analogue format.

8. One of the heuristic devices which I utilize throughout this book is the notion of the gap. MacDougall (1998) suggests that viewing subjects insert themselves into the gaps in film's montage. In my reading, the gap allows us to think about the ways in which a viewer might be called into the work, without recourse to notions of interpellation and theories of identification in the cinema. It suggests that the viewer slips through the cracks and is inserted into the fabric of the film. It suggests also an interaction between the life on-screen and a life off-screen. The gap is the space which holds the film together—and grants the film its possibility—but is itself not fully visible.

9. The periodization is not complete. Certain discrete elements of fashion are contemporary and there is the presence of the spectators at the end. Ramesar was not aiming to isolate the figures in a frozen past (Ramesar 2005).

10. The title of the article discussed here (Føllesdal 2003).

11. Dreyfus (1972) discusses the fundamental disagreement in commentaries on Husserl over what was intended by the term "perceptual noema." He points to two strands of interpretation: Føllesdal's noema as concept and Gurwitsch's noema as percept, or object of perception. See Zahavi (2003) for a discussion of "East coast" and "West coast" interpretations of the noema in US scholarship. While there is considerable debate concerning what Husserl may have intended by his use of the term "noema," the idea of individual components of an act of consciousness—each playing a different role in the presentation of objects to consciousness—is of strategic value here.

12. Musical instrument also known as maracas.

13. Although the ceremony takes place at a delta it is the river, rather than its approach to the sea, that is most evident here.

14. This work is the result of a collaboration between Robert Yao Ramesar and Sonja Melton Ramesar. The main scene is an Orisha festival dedicated to Oshun, the Goddess of the river. The deliberately over-exposed images in Mami Wata, producing many of the "washes", were shot principally by Sonja Melton Ramesar. The images of higher contrast, foregrounding shadow and detail, were shot principally by Ramesar. The slow motion edit, for which Ramesar was responsible, adds a dreamlike quality to the entire piece.

15. I take these terms for objects appearing inside the mind (thoughts) and outside the mind from Husserl (1999). Although Depraz does not use these terms specifically, they are certainly relevant here.

16. Spirit possession has received considerable attention in the anthropological literature and some attention in film scholarship. Such studies are generally concerned with conveying the experience of possession rather than the experience of watching spirit *come to visibility* through the medium of film or video. Film scholar Catherine Russell (1999, 2003) examines the work of Maya Deren on possession in Haitian *vodou* and finds that it is unsuccessful, in part, because the gap between the experience of possession and its cinematic representation is unbridgeable. The excessive nature of possession renders it in some way unrepresentable. Russell suggests that the body in trance becomes a signifier without a referent. In *Mami Wata*, it is precisely this excess that renders the experience tangible as an appearing.

17. According to Alweiss (2003), Heidegger's approach negates the world entirely, whereas Husserl acknowledges the world and places it strategically in suspension so that we may return to it with renewed and more critical perception. This is what I characterize as the fulfilment of Husserl's intention.

18. I take the notion of boundary condition from Føllesdal (2003) who, in his discussion of the thetic role of consciousness, suggests that the hyle or present sensations provide a boundary condition for our experience.

19. Mother Ganga, the river Ganges.

20. Small clay lamps.

21. A form of ritual devotion in Hindu tradition characterized by repetitive circular movements of lighted deyas on a brass or copper plate.

22. A brass pitcher.

23. A sacred paste.

24. Ramesar has indicated that the sound for this video was recorded on the day of the festival. It is the singing of a pundit along the festival route. He encountered the pundit singing in a cave (Ramesar 2005). The echo in the original recording resonates with the tone of the video.

25. Carlson (2007) discusses givenness in the context of Jean-Luc Marion's saturated phenomenon and the question of revelation. He discusses the call in Marion (1997) as a given which exists before the Dasein and before the intention of the called. Although Carlson is describing a phenomenon far more subtle and complex than can be discussed here, the notion of irreducible givenness seems appropriate to the interpretation of *Journey to Ganga Mai* as the ultimate reduction that exists beyond our own subjective acts of consciousness and intention.

Bibliography

Alweiss, L. *The World Unclaimed: A Challenge to Heidegger's Critique of Husserl*. Athens, OH: Ohio University Press, 2003.

Andrew, D. *Concepts in Film Theory*. Oxford, UK: Oxford University Press, 1984.

———. "The Neglected Tradition of Phenomenology in Film Theory." In B. Nichols (ed.), *Movies and Methods: An Anthology Volume II* (Berkeley, CA: University of California Press, 1985), pp. 625–632.

Andrew, J. D. *The Major Film Theories: An Introduction*. New York, NY: Oxford University Press, 1976.

Ayfre, A. *Le cinéma et sa vérité*. Paris, France: Les Editions du Cerf, 1969.

Bergson, H. *Duration and Simultaneity: With Reference to Einstein's Theory*, translated by L. Jacobson. Indianapolis, IN: Bobbs-Merrill Company, Inc., 1965.

———. *Matter and Memory*, translated by N. M. Paul and W. S. Palmer. New York, NY: Zone Books, 1988.

Bhabha, H. K. *The Location of Culture*. London, UK: Routledge, 1994.

Carlson, T. A. "Blindness and the Decision to See: On Revelation and Reception in Jean-Luc Marion." In K. Hart (ed.), *Counter-Experiences: Reading Jean-Luc Marion* (Notre Dame, IN: University of Notre Dame Press, 2007), 153–179.

Cham, M. (ed.). *Ex-iles: Essays on Caribbean Cinema*. Trenton, NJ: Africa World Press, 1992.

Chion, M. "Projections of Sound on Image." In R. Stam and T. Miller (eds.), *Film and Theory: An Anthology* (Malden, MA: Blackwell Publishing, 2000), pp. 111–124.

Costa, V. "Transcendental Aesthetic and the Problem of Transcendentality." In N. Depraz and D. Zahavi (eds.), *Alterity and Facticity: New Perspectives on Husserl* (Dordrecht, Netherlands: Kluwer Academic Publishers, 1998), pp. 9–28.

Deger, J. *Shimmering Screens: Making Media in an Aboriginal Community*. Minneapolis, MN: University of Minnesota Press, 2006.

Depraz, N. "The Phenomenological Reduction as Praxis." In F. J. Varela and J. Shear (eds.), *The View from Within: First-person Approaches to the Study of Consciousness* (Thorverton, UK: Imprint Academic, 1999), pp. 95–110.

Dreyfus, H. L. "The Perceptual Noema: Gurwitsch's Contribution." In L. Embree (ed.), *Life-World and Consciousness: Essays for Aron Gurwitsch* (Evanston, IL: Northwestern University Press), pp. 135–170.

Føllesdal, D. "The Thetic Role of Consciousness." In D. Fisette (ed.), *Husserl's Logical Investigations Reconsidered* (Dordrecht, Netherlands: Kluwer Academic Publishers, 2003), pp. 11–20.

Gabriel, T. H. *Third Cinema in the Third World: The Aesthetic of Liberation*. Ann Arbor, MI: UMI Research Press, 1982.

Gabriel, T. H. "Towards a Critical Theory of Third World Films." In J. Pines and P. Willemen (eds.), *Questions of Third Cinema* (London, UK: BFI, 1989), pp. 3–51.

Gurwitsch, A. "Husserl's Theory of the Intentionality of Consciousness in Historical Perspective." In E. N. Lee and M. Mandelbaum (eds.), *Phenomenology and Existentialism* (Baltimore, MD: The Johns Hopkins University Press, 1967), pp. 25–27.

Heidegger, M. *The Basic Problems of Phenomenology*, translated by A. Hofstadter, edited by J. M. Edie. Bloomington, IN: Indiana University Press, 1988.

———. *Zollicon Seminars: Protocols-Conversations-Letters*, edited by M. Boss. Evanston, IL: Northwestern University Press, 2001.

Husserl, E. *The Idea of Phenomenology*, translated by L. Hardy. Dordrecht, Netherlands: Kluwer Academic Publishers, 1999.

Ihde, D. *Sense and Significance*. Pittsburgh, PA: Duquesne University Press, (distributed by Humanities Press, New York, NY), 1973.

———. *Listening and Voice: A Phenomenology of Sound*. Athens, OH: Ohio University Press, 1976.

———. *Experimental Phenomenology: An Introduction*. Albany, NY: State University of New York, 1986.

Lovitt, W. "Introduction." In M. Heidegger, *The Question Concerning Technology and Other Essays*, translated by W. Lovitt (New York, NY: Harper and Row, 1977), pp. 13–39.

MacDougall, D. *Transcultural Cinema*. Princeton, NJ: Princeton University Press, 1998.

Mahabir, K. *A Dictionary of Common Trinidad Hindi*. San Juan, Trinidad and Tobago: Chakra Publishing House (Caribbean), 2004.

Marion, J.-L. *Etant donné: essai d'une phénoménologie de la donation*. Paris, France: Presses Universitaires de France, 1997.

Marks, L. U. *The Skin of the Film: Intercultural Cinema, Embodiment, and the Senses*. Durham, NC: Duke University Press, 2000.

———. "How Electrons Remember." In L. U. Marks, *Touch: Sensuous Theory and Multisensory Media* (Minneapolis, MN: University of Minnesota Press, 2002), pp. 161–176.

Maxwell, M. A. O. "Magical Realism Television: Theatre as Counter Media." *Trinidad and Tobago Review* (August 1998), pp. 20–21, 23–24.

———. "Yao Makes Us See." *Trinidad and Tobago Review* (November 2000), pp. 27–28.

McLure, R. *The Philosophy of Time: Time Before Times*. London, UK: Routledge, 2005.

Melton Ramesar, S., Personal communication with the author. 6 July, 2009.

Meunier, J.-P. *Les structures de l'expérience filmique: l'identification filmique*. Louvain, Belgium: Les Presses Universitaires, 1969.

Merleau-Ponty, M. *The Visible and the Invisible (Followed by Working Notes)*, translated by A. Lingis, edited by C. Lefort. Evanston, IL: Northwestern University Press, 1968.

———. *Phenomenology, Language and Sociology: Selected Essays of Maurice Merleau-Ponty*, edited by J. O'Neill. London, UK: Heinemann Educational Books, 1974.

Ramesar, R. Y. "Caribbeing: Cultural Imperatives and the Technology of Motion Picture Production." *Caribbean Quarterly* 41:4 (1996), pp. 19–21.

————. "Caribbeing: Technique and Technology in Caribbean Still & Motion Picture Aesthetics." Paper presented at *The Caribbean, Towards 2000— Models for Multi-Cultural Arts Education*. St. Augustine, Trinidad and Tobago: The Festival Centre for the Creative Arts, The University of the West Indies, 1997.

————. Discussion with the author. 10 August 2003.

————. Interview with the author. 5 September 2004.

————. Interview with the author. 25 June 2005.

Rony, F. T. *The Third Eye: Race, Cinema, and Ethnographic Spectacle*. Durham, NC: Duke University Press, 1996.

Rouch, J. "On the Vicissitudes of the Self: The Possessed, the Dancer, the Magician, the Sorcerer, the Filmmaker, and the Ethnographer." In J. Rouch, *Ciné-Ethnography*, edited and translated by S. Feld (Minneapolis, MN: University of Minnesota Press, 2003), pp. 87–101.

————. "Ciné-Anthropology," with E. Fulchignoni. In J. Rouch, *Ciné-Ethnography*, edited and translated by S. Feld (Minneapolis, MN: University of Minnesota Press, 2003), pp. 147–187.

————. "*Les maîtres fous*, *The Lion Hunters*, and *Jaguar*," with J. Marshall and J.W. Adams. In J. Rouch, *Ciné-Ethnography*, edited and translated by S. Feld (Minneapolis, MN: University of Minnesota Press), pp. 188– 209.

Russell, C. *Experimental Ethnography: The Work of Film in the Age of Video*. Durham, NC: Duke University Press, 1999.

————. "Ecstatic Ethnography: Maya Deren and the Filming of Possession." In I. Margulies (ed.), *Rites of Realism: Essays on Corporeal Cinema* (Durham, NC: Duke University Press, 2003), pp. 270–293.

So, D. C. C. *A Phenomenological Study of the Mysticism of St. John of the Cross.* PhD dissertation, McMaster University, 2001.

Sobchack, V. *The Address of the Eye: A Phenomenology of Film Experience.* Princeton, NJ: Princeton University Press, 1992.

———. "Toward a Phenomenology of Non-fictional Film Experience." In J. Gaines and M. Renov (eds.), *Collecting Visible Evidence* (Minneapolis, MN: University of Minnesota Press, 1999), pp. 241–254.

Tarkovsky, A. *Sculpting in Time*, translated by K. Hunter-Blair. Austin, TX: University of Texas Press, 1986.

Trinh, T. M.-H. *When the Moon Waxes Red: Representation, Gender and Cultural Politics.* New York, NY: Routledge, 1991.

———. *Framer Framed.* New York, NY: Routledge, 1992.

———. *Cinema Interval.* New York, NY: Routledge, 1999.

Warner, K. Q. *On Location: Cinema and Film in the Anglophone Caribbean.* London, UK: Macmillan, 2000.

Young, J. *Heidegger's Later Philosophy.* Cambridge, UK: Cambridge University Press, 2002.

Zahavi, D. *Husserl's Phenomenology.* Stanford, CA: Stanford University Press, 2003.

Videography

Heritage: A Wedding in Moriah. Robert Yao Ramesar. Trinidad and Tobago, 1997, 12 min., video.

Journey to Ganga Mai. Robert Yao Ramesar. Trinidad and Tobago, 1999, 10 min., video.

Mami Wata. Robert Yao Ramesar and Sonja Melton. Trinidad and Tobago, 1996 [1992], 10 min., video.

Parlour People. Robert Yao Ramesar. Trinidad and Tobago, 1996, 8 min., video.